International Law: A Very Short Introduction

Titles in the series include the following:

ACCOUNTING Christopher Nobes
ADOLESCENCE Peter K. Smith
ADVERTISING Winston Fletcher
AFRICAN AMERICAN RELIGION
    Eddie S. Glaude Jr
AFRICAN HISTORY John Parker and
    Richard Rathbone
AFRICAN RELIGIONS
    Jacob K. Olupona
AGEING Nancy A. Pachana
AGNOSTICISM Robin Le Poidevin
AGRICULTURE Paul Brassley and
    Richard Soffe
ALEXANDER THE GREAT
    Hugh Bowden
ALGEBRA Peter M. Higgins
AMERICAN HISTORY Paul S. Boyer
AMERICAN IMMIGRATION
    David A. Gerber
AMERICAN LEGAL HISTORY
    G. Edward White
AMERICAN POLITICAL
    HISTORY Donald Critchlow
AMERICAN POLITICAL PARTIES
    AND ELECTIONS L. Sandy Maisel
AMERICAN POLITICS
    Richard M. Valelly
THE AMERICAN
    PRESIDENCY Charles O. Jones
THE AMERICAN REVOLUTION
    Robert J. Allison
AMERICAN SLAVERY
    Heather Andrea Williams
THE AMERICAN WEST Stephen Aron

AMERICAN WOMEN'S HISTORY
    Susan Ware
ANAESTHESIA Aidan O'Donnell
ANARCHISM Colin Ward
ANCIENT ASSYRIA Karen Radner
ANCIENT EGYPT Ian Shaw
ANCIENT EGYPTIAN ART AND
    ARCHITECTURE Christina Riggs
ANCIENT GREECE Paul Cartledge
THE ANCIENT NEAR EAST
    Amanda H. Podany
ANCIENT PHILOSOPHY Julia Annas
ANCIENT WARFARE Harry Sidebottom
ANGELS David Albert Jones
ANGLICANISM Mark Chapman
THE ANGLO-SAXON AGE
    John Blair
ANIMAL BEHAVIOUR
    Tristram D. Wyatt
THE ANIMAL KINGDOM
    Peter Holland
ANIMAL RIGHTS David DeGrazia
THE ANTARCTIC Klaus Dodds
ANTISEMITISM Steven Beller
ANXIETY Daniel Freeman and
    Jason Freeman
THE APOCRYPHAL GOSPELS
    Paul Foster
ARCHAEOLOGY Paul Bahn
ARCHITECTURE Andrew Ballantyne
ARISTOCRACY William Doyle
ARISTOTLE Jonathan Barnes
ART HISTORY Dana Arnold
ART THEORY Cynthia Freeland

Vaughan Lowe

INTERNATIONAL
LAW

A Very Short Introduction

OXFORD
UNIVERSITY PRESS

OXFORD
UNIVERSITY PRESS

Great Clarendon Street, Oxford, OX2 6DP,
United Kingdom

Oxford University Press is a department of the University of Oxford.
It furthers the University's objective of excellence in research, scholarship,
and education by publishing worldwide. Oxford is a registered trade mark of
Oxford University Press in the UK and in certain other countries

First edition published in 2015

Published in the United States of America by Oxford University Press
198 Madison Avenue, New York, NY 10016, United States of America

British Library Cataloguing in Publication Data
Data available

Library of Congress Control Number: 2015909030

ISBN 978-0-19-923933-7

Printed and bound by
CPI Group (UK) Ltd, Croydon, CR0 4YY

Contents

List of illustrations

Chapter 1
Nations under law

Man is born in chains: but everywhere thinks himself free. None of us could survive for long—let alone lead a productive and rewarding life—if we suddenly had to provide our own food, drink, power, clothing, and so on, without the assistance of others. Those of us who live in urban environments are particularly dependent upon others who provide the services and technology which, barely noticed, support our lives. The debt and dependence is, indeed, an intergenerational matter. We may know that we can make fire by rubbing sticks together, iron by smelting, and microchips by using computerized machines; but were we to start from the raw materials that the earth provides, the process of making tools to mine the earth, building engines to power industrialized production, and achieving the level of mechanical precision and intellectual skill necessary to progress to the manufacture of, say, a microchip would not only take far longer than any one lifetime, it would probably outstrip mankind's social ability to organize long-term projects. Our civilization is held together by a fragile web of interdependence.

It is obvious that man is a social animal, who can survive only in a society—that every individual is chained to a society as a necessary condition of his or her individual survival. The existence of what some think of as the personal wealth, possessions, and entitlements of an individual is in truth possible only by virtue of the collaboration of all the other individuals who make up that society. Yet it is equally clear that one of the most powerful of the forces driving both individual and social development is the idea of freedom, whether as a goal, an aspiration, a principle, a right, a duty, or in some other didactic role. This relationship between freedom and society is epitomized in the national anthems of the world. These are the words that governments like us to sing in order to affirm our solidarity, our identity as a 'people', and, of course, our allegiance to our governments: and 'freedom' is by far the most common theme to be found in these anthems.

The contrast between the fact of the radical dependence of individuals upon society and the pervasive assertion of freedom may seem a trite observation. Fundamental truths often do: their interest lies in working out their implications and corollaries. The significant corollary here is that the function of international law, at the most basic level, is to secure the coexistence of sovereign States. It creates the ordering of societies and of relationships between societies, and the body of rules and principles, through which the paradox of the chained man's defiant affirmation of his freedom is worked out on the international scale (see Figure 1).

The myth of the sovereign State

International lawyers naturally think of that ordering in terms of relations between States. Whatever the nature of the State, whether it is a democracy or a theocracy, liberal or repressive, egalitarian or elitist or whatever, it is the State which stands as the most prominent social unit within which the rules and values that are the main external constraints on individual action are articulated.

The focus upon the State is a working assumption, a matter of choice and characterization, rather than a conclusion derived from the observation of how people around the world in fact relate

2

1. What rules are necessary to ensure that States can coexist?

to one another. In practice, people organize themselves in, or join, or are born into, a range of different groups: families, tribes, cities, professions, religions, denominations, political parties, provinces, nations, confederations, States, regions, and so on—though not endless, the list is lengthy. Individual identities are the products of combinations of these allegiances, and of the abandonment or rejection of such allegiances.

If, at some time or in some context, the most influential and relevant distinction were that focused upon what city or region we live in, or our religious affiliation, or what football team we support or what computer operating system we use, we would expect to see the daily news and political debate and written

3

histories that constitute the public narrative of social life to be constructed to reflect that different focus. Indeed, it is normal for such different focuses to coexist: local news programmes come after the national and international news on the television; national newspapers, local newspapers, and gossip reflect the different circles of our social interests. Anyone who lives solely on one plane of social life is probably a saint or an obsessive bore. But, at least for those concerned with international affairs, whose view of the world is formed by national or international newspapers and television, the primary unit of political and economic organization is still the State—the independent sovereign State, whose essence is that it is subject to the authority of no other body, and that its relations with other groups are a matter of its consent and agreement rather than of obligation and direction by some other body to which it is subordinate.

This independence enjoyed by States manifests itself most obviously as a matter of political principle. Those in power routinely affirm and observe the principles of the sovereign equality and independence of States in their dealings with those in other countries. These principles determine who can routinely tell whom to do what, with the expectation of obedience driven by a sense of obligation. The police, local government agencies, the army, and so on routinely obey the laws and orders laid down by the central government of their own State, and not the laws and orders of any other State or body. Instructions emanating from other quarters are taken as signs of a 'loss of sovereignty', much as medieval doctors took irritability and envy as signs of a surplus of bile. Sovereignty means that all States are equal: each has the right not to be dictated to by the others.

In practice, of course, the position is different. Many States around the world commonly defer to the wishes of a local, regional, or global superpower—much as individuals who have in principle the dignity of independence and equality before the law tend to show a particular regard for the wishes of employers, police officers, hostage-takers, and others in a position to do them significant good or significant harm.

The size and the boundaries of the social group that is treated as an independent State are themselves somewhat arbitrary. Whole groups of what might have taken the form of separate States have come together under the umbrella of a single State. The individual states, such as Hawaii, California, Alaska, and New Hampshire, which make up the United States of America provide one example. The individual republics, such as Georgia, Azerbaijan, Russia, and Belarus, which, until 1991, made up the USSR, offer another. Conversely, the break-up of the USSR, and Yugoslavia, and Sudan has demonstrated that a single State that has existed for many years may fragment into smaller units.

It is the arbitrariness of these groupings that lies behind many international conflicts. Chechen separatists think that Chechnya should not be wrapped in as part of Russia; Tamil Tigers thought that there should be a separate State of Tamil Eelam in the north of Sri Lanka; Ukrainian separatists wish to break away from Ukraine and reunite with Russia. There are, on the other hand, those who think that a federal project should be pursued within Europe, welding the Member States of the European Union into a single federal State.

The separation and combination of social units, whatever their scale or nature, is rarely revolutionary. It usually takes place through gradual transfers of particular powers between governmental authorities: devolution of certain powers from central to local government, transfers of powers from Member States to the European Commission, and so on. Over time, some units become more important, and others less so. The waxing and waning of the relative powers of cities, principalities, States, and the EU in Europe over the past thousand years is a good example.

The relations between these and other social units are addressed by various bodies of law. Constitutional law looks at the internal structure of the State and matters such as the relationship between central and local government; EU law looks at the structure of the EU and its relationship with the governments, legislatures, and courts of Member States, and at its outward relations with non-EU States; and so on. International law focuses on the relationship between independent sovereign States. It is one among many cross-sections that can be cut through the structures of social and political life.

Sovereign equality

The idea of the sovereign State is one of the mythical principles that have underpinned political life for the past two or three centuries, since the decline of the ordering of political relations upon the basis of empires, religious or secular. The idea of sovereignty—or, more precisely, of sovereign equality—is the international equivalent of the principle that men are born and remain free and equal in rights—or, as one lapel badge has it, 'remember you're unique; just like everyone else'. In international law, this principle is reflected in Article 2 of the UN Charter, which records that the UN 'is based on the principle of the sovereign equality of all of its Members'.

China (estimated population in 2014, according to the *CIA Factbook*, 1,356 million; approximate area 9.6 million square kilometres) and Nauru (estimated population 9,488; approximate area 21 square kilometres) are equal sovereign States, and each of them has one vote as a Member State in the UN General Assembly. China can no more compel Nauru to sign up to, say, the Convention on Climate Change than Nauru can compel China to do so—though both States have in fact chosen to become parties to that particular treaty. As in human life, vast differences in power and wealth are not allowed to extinguish the principle that in the eyes of the law (if nowhere else) neither can force its will upon the other.

The real value of the principle of sovereign equality to any particular State is an interesting question; but its importance to the international legal system is very great. It generates the fundamental features of the architecture of the system.

Every State is free to make treaties with other States, and no treaty is binding upon a State unless it has agreed to become a party to it. Every State may by its conduct seek to initiate a new rule of customary international law. In the great majority of international organizations where decisions are taken by majority vote, the vote of each State is equal. (There are exceptions, such as the International Monetary Fund and the European Union, in which votes are weighted to reflect the relative importance of States within the context of the activities of the organization: i.e. the relative international importance of their economies.) Every State is entitled to the same degree of immunity for its actions and for its diplomats from the jurisdiction of the courts of every other State. And so on.

Some States are, of course, very much more active and influential than others. But even small States can have a considerable influence. Malta played a crucial role in the major reform of the law of the sea, which governs the legal regime for 70 per cent of the area of the globe, in the 1980s; and some of the most significant developments in that area of the law in earlier years had been initiated by States such as Peru, Chile, and Ecuador. A good deal depends upon the personal qualities of the representatives of the State. A visionary and skilled ambassador or Foreign Minister can wield an influence wholly disproportionate to the size of the State that he or she represents. But in a world where ideas are disseminated with astonishing rapidity, it may matter little who first articulates a concept that meets the need of the time. Who now remembers the origins of the calls for treaties for the repression of bribery or torture or government subsidies for exports?

The implications of the principle of sovereign equality are worked out in specific rules of international law. For example, the Vienna Convention on the Law of Treaties stipulates that treaties procured by coercion are void, thus reflecting the principle that each State must freely give its consent to be bound by a treaty and that no State has the right to impose its will on another. There are, as will be seen in the following pages, prohibitions on the threat or use of force by one State against any other State, and upon economic coercion. More subtly, the equality of States is protected by the principles governing the jurisdiction of States—the extent to which a State can subject people and transactions to its laws and its courts. These principles protect the ability of each State to decide for itself what kind of society it will seek to maintain within its borders through the operation of its own domestic law (or 'municipal law', as the law applicable within a State or part of a State—e.g. English law or Scots law—is sometimes called).

The centrality of the State in the international legal system leads to a commonly held view that the history of international law runs parallel with the history of the State as a political concept. The modern State system is sometimes said to date from the Peace of Westphalia in the mid-17th century, or from the rise of the Italian city-States during the Renaissance; and international law is said to have found its feet as a scholarly and professional discipline in the works of Hugo Grotius, the 17th-century Dutch polymath and diplomat, and his successors such as Emerich de Vattel. That is rather hard on writers such as Alberico Gentili, an Oxford professor whose work precedes and more than matches that of Grotius for its legal sophistication, and even earlier jurists such as Vitoria and Suarez, who debated the legal aspects of the Spanish imperial conquest of the new world. But such potted histories miss the point, in three main ways.

First, there have always been intercommunal relations. Even before the European system of independent States became the norm, empires dealt with neighbouring empires and States and vassals. Second, there is outside Europe a rich, and much older, history of writings that are as much 'international law' as the writings of Grotius. The work of the 9th-century Iraqi jurist Shaybānī, and the Indian Kautilya, more than a thousand years earlier, are the best known. And, third, books are in my view the wrong focus. It is bureaucracy and habit that carries the soul of international law; lawyers merely systematize it. There is a continuity in the principles and rituals applied in dealings between 21st-century States that can be traced back to the earliest dealings of diplomats and agents and messengers moving between political communities. Ancient Babylonian treaties are recognizably the same kinds of act and instrument as modern treaties. If a beginning is sought for international law, it lies at the time that a professional assistant to some chief or king first recorded for the benefit of other officials the promises made by foreign rulers and ways of dealing with foreign communities (including 'proper' ways of waging war against them).

States and peoples

The world is currently divided up among almost 200 sovereign States. The number is approximate because from time to time old States disappear and new States emerge. Malaysia and the United Arab Emirates, for example, were formed by the federation of States that had, earlier in their histories and prior to periods of colonial rule, been independent. Conversely, many new States emerged during the years of decolonization, when former colonies gained their independence from the Great Powers which had previously conducted the international relations of what were sometimes called their 'overseas possessions'.

Decolonization is the main reason that the number of sovereign States has more than trebled since 1945. Other States emerged from the break-up of what had become (often as a result of the earlier fusion of independent states or principalities) single States, such as the Soviet Union and Yugoslavia.

Such States can at least be counted; but there are also entities such as the 'Turkish Republic of Northern Cyprus' (the 'TRNC') and, formerly, the South African Bantustans such as Transkei and Ciskei which have claimed to be States but have been recognized by no States other than the State (Turkey, and South Africa, respectively) which purported to establish them. Similarly, there are entities such as Palestine and Kosovo, which assert their Statehood and are recognized by many, but not (yet) by all other States. The position of such entities is often unclear; but the lack of clarity arises primarily from the unwillingness of some or all States to accept what are usually clear conclusions that would result from the impartial application of rules of international law. It is political opposition that keeps Palestine out of the United Nations, for example, and not any failure to fulfil the legal conditions for Statehood.

As a matter of international law, in order to be a State it is necessary for an entity to have a permanent population. One reason that Antarctica could not be a sovereign State is that it has no inhabitants: it has only visiting scientists and tourists. (The general view is that Antarctica is owned by no one; but a handful of States including the UK, France, and Australia lay claim to parts of it.) The population must also be organized under an effective government, able to command or compel the obedience of most of the people most of the time. It is a central purpose of a system of States that dealings among them should be conducted on the basis that there is one effective authority to represent each and every society and area on the planet, with the rights and responsibilities that flow from that premise.

The requirement that each State must have a physical territory, even if very small, is one of the essential conditions of Statehood under international law. Lands originally came under the rule of a particular sovereign by conquest; and conquest was recognized until the first part of the 20th century as a lawful means of acquiring territory. Nowadays title to territory can change only by peaceful means, such as the cession of the territory by treaty, or the long and unchallenged occupation of territory that can give rise to a title based upon prescription. It is not necessary that the entire course of the borders of a State should be precisely fixed. Israel was recognized as a State before its borders were wholly settled, as was India. But there must be a clear view that there is a State in existence in a particular location, even if its exact boundaries may remain to be determined.

No matter how refined the virtual worlds of cyberspace might be, they do not feature on the map of international relations. One should be cautious, however, in dismissing the possibility that virtual States might emerge. The Vatican City is accepted as a sovereign State, despite its tiny size (listed as zero in the *CIA World Factbook*, but in fact about 0.44 square kilometres) and small population (estimated as 842, and unlikely to be self-sustaining). Its modern Statehood was established by the 1929 Lateran Treaty; and the Holy See—a distinct juridical person which coexists with and has its seat in the State of Vatican City—is perceived as the representative of Roman Catholics (or perhaps more accurately of Roman Catholicism) worldwide. The Vatican City may be explained as an anomalous historical survival; but it appears to be generally accepted that it may continue to exercise its Statehood. There is no characteristic of Roman Catholicism that would today demand that level of representation in a way that, say, Islam or Hinduism would not; and it is difficult to see why a similar case should not be made out for the representation of other, non-religious, virtual societies. At present, however, every State needs a physical basis. Along with a permanent population and an effective government, territory is one of the criteria of legal Statehood.

There is generally said to be a fourth criterion: the capacity to enter into relations with other States, which is understood to require that the entity be free to decide upon and to conduct its own foreign policies, and not be subject to control by any other State—another manifestation of the sovereign equality principle. It is this last requirement of independence that explains why the 'TRNC' is not, and the South African Bantustans were not, recognized as States: they are considered to be wholly dependent upon Turkey and South Africa respectively.

Some States, and some international lawyers, take the view that there is also a fifth requirement, of what might be called 'legitimacy': that the entity has achieved the requisite independence in a manner consistent with international law. That offers another explanation for the non-recognition of the 'TRNC' and the Bantustans. The former was the product of the 1974 armed invasion of Cyprus by Turkey, and the latter of the implementation of the policy of apartheid, both being regarded by practically all other States as violations of international law. The question of the need for 'legitimacy' remains without a definitive answer, because it is a question that is unlikely to come before a tribunal for decision (although aspects of it arose in a 2010 Advisory Opinion of the International Court of Justice concerning the status of Kosovo). Judges in national courts will in practice follow the lead of their governments, which rarely explain why they do or do not recognize a new State; and on the international plane, the decision is in practice taken by the vote of the General Assembly acting on the recommendation of the Security Council, on an application by the putative State for UN membership—an application unlikely to be made until the candidate feels that it has sufficient support to succeed.

Self-determination

Those are the requirements of Statehood: the criteria that must be met if an entity wishes to be treated as a State. International law contains an important principle that gives a positive right to

Statehood. This is 'the principle of equal rights and self-determination of peoples', enshrined in Article 1 of the UN Charter. Often traced back to early Marxist texts such as the resolution on 'the full right of all nations to self-determination [*Selbstbestimmungsrecht*]' adopted by the 1896 London International Congress, it is difficult to separate self-determination from nationalism. The essence of the legal principle is that no people should be subject to alien domination, particularly of the colonial variety.

That is not to say that self-determination necessarily entails independence. A people may choose independence, but they may choose some form of free association with an independent State or even integration with an independent State. The people of the Falkland Islands/Malvinas and of Gibraltar, whom the British government regard as having the right of self-determination, remain British territories as a matter of choice, as determined by referenda on the subject.

The principle of self-determination attaches to a 'people'. Shared and distinct ethnicity, language, culture, and history are the kinds of characteristics that identify a 'people'. The Finns and the Saharwi, for example, are 'peoples'. In 1960, UN General Assembly resolution 1514 (XV) (the 'XV' refers to the annual session of the UN, measured from the date of its establishment in 1945), on the granting of independence to colonial countries and peoples, supplemented by resolution 1541 on the duty of States to develop self-government within any non-self-governing territories for which they were responsible, spelled out some of the details of the right of self-determination. There is, however, no authoritative definition of a 'people', although expert bodies have recommended criteria for determining 'peoplehood' and detailed analyses of the question have accompanied the decisions made in the context of events such as the break-up of Yugoslavia.

The reason for the lack of an authoritative definition is the acutely controversial nature of the question. Argentina and Spain have taken the view that 'planted' populations, such as those in the Malvinas/Falkland Islands and in Gibraltar, do not have a right of self-determination. Given the vagaries of human history, the idea that only autochthonous populations, rooted in the territory, have the right would severely limit the scope of self-determination, as consideration of the position of countries such as the USA and England makes clear. The objections to 'planted' populations are better seen as objections to particular vestiges of the colonial period.

There is a further and clearer qualification to the right of self-determination. UN General Assembly resolution 2625 (XXV)—the Declaration on Principles of International Law concerning Friendly Relations and Cooperation Among States in Accordance with the Charter of the United Nations—which was adopted by consensus in 1970, reflected the general understanding of States in stipulating that the right of self-determination does not authorize or encourage any action that would impair the territorial integrity or political unity of existing sovereign and independent States. While all States could agree upon the desirability of ending European colonialism, none wished to see the principle drafted in terms that would encourage domestic secessionist movements, such as the Basques, Tamils, Chechens, Scots, and many others, by giving them a legal right to secede (see Figure 2). It is not that such groups are denied all legal recognition; but they are treated as minorities entitled to special protection within States, sometimes under legal instruments such as the 1995 European Framework Convention on National Minorities, rather than as 'peoples' entitled to the right of self-determination.

Recognition of States and governments

Entities may fulfil the criteria for Statehood. Their people may, in addition, have the right of self-determination. But they may not be recognized as a State. Palestine is the most obvious example. The establishment by the UN in 1975 of the Committee on

2. **The Basques are among the claimants to self-determination. This mural was painted on a wall in republican Belfast.**

the Exercise of the Inalienable Rights of the Palestinian People clearly affirmed the right of the Palestinian people to self-determination; and the requirements of a permanent population, a territory with reasonably clearly defined borders, an effective government, and independence from other States are at least arguably as well met as they were in the case of some other entities when they were admitted to the UN as States. (While Israel is in military occupation of parts of Palestinian territory, Israel claims sovereignty only over certain parts of Palestinian territory—notably around Jerusalem—and does not claim that Palestine as a whole is legally subject to Israeli rule.) Yet Palestine is still not recognized as a State by the USA, Israel, and some other States, and has, indeed, had sanctions imposed upon it by Israel for having sought admission to the UN unilaterally and outside the framework of a comprehensive settlement with Israel of the Palestinian question.

The explanation for this paradoxical position is that although the legal criteria for Statehood may clearly be met, no entity can compel another to recognize it as a State. Recognition remains a high political act; and one State may refuse to recognize another purely as a matter of political discretion. A State may decide that at a given time political stability and justice are better served by non-recognition, as some States do not recognize Palestine and several States refuse to recognize Israel, although both of them meet the legal criteria of Statehood. Recognition is withheld in the hope of mounting pressure for a durable political settlement.

Recognition of one State by another is usually signalled by some formal step such as the exchange of diplomatic representatives: non-recognition is signalled by steps such as refusals to accept an unrecognized State as a party to an international treaty or to allow diplomatic representation of the entity, as well as by express statements.

An unrecognized State that fulfils the objective criteria of Statehood cannot, however, be treated as non-existent. No State is entitled to invade the territory of an unrecognized State, for example. But one State can refuse to have any State-to-State dealings with another—any normal diplomatic relations—and States are allowed a wide (but not unlimited) discretion in deciding whether to support or oppose an application from an entity to become a Member State in the United Nations and other international bodies that are open only to States.

In the past it was not unusual explicitly to grant recognition to foreign governments as well as to States, in circumstances where a new government came to power by non-constitutional means—by a coup, for example, rather than via elections. That practice was abandoned in the course of the 20th century by most States, primarily because it was thought inappropriate for one State to purport to 'approve' the government of another, and because it was feared that recognition in any particular case might be interpreted by the rest of the world as approval of a regime that might well have come to power through some unusually toxic combination of thuggery and corruption.

As a matter of policy the UK formally abandoned the recognition of foreign governments in 1980, announcing the policy change in parliamentary statements. Unaccountably, it reverted to its earlier practice in 2011, when it announced that it would henceforth recognize the 'rebel' government in the nascent Libyan civil war as the legitimate government, and by implication de-recognize the incumbent government in Tripoli—an announcement about as appropriate and helpful as applause at the end of the second movement of a string quartet.

Non-recognition cannot deprive a government of its basic entitlements, for example to some measure of respect for laws that it has enacted and acts that it has undertaken within the territory that it controls. It can, however, make life very difficult. An unrecognized government may be unable to access the State's bank accounts, or occupy the State's seat in international organizations, for example; and more broadly, the political and economic impact of a refusal to treat a foreign regime as a legitimate government can severely limit its ability to participate in international relations.

Back to the plot

The short point is that, viewed politically, the world is divided up (for the most part uncontroversially) into States in just the way that is depicted in coloured school atlases. These States are the repositories of the sovereign independence which gives those who govern the States the right to choose and determine the nature of the social order which prevails within them, to the extent that the

social order is established or underwritten by laws and by
government action.

It is with these States, and the relations between them, that
international law deals. International law provides for the security
of their borders, and for their right to be free from invasion and
coercion by neighbouring States. It underpins the right of each
State to choose its political, economic, and social structures. It
provides mechanisms and procedures for the conduct of relations
between States across the whole range of economic, political, and
diplomatic activity; and it also provides the framework within
which individual citizens can choose to travel and engage in
transactions across national borders, whether in relation to trade,
marriage, tourism, organized crime, or some other focus of human
ingenuity and enterprise. And by regulating the scope of a State's
jurisdiction—its right to make and enforce laws that say what
people may and may not do, and how, when, where, and with
whom they may do it—it determines the effective scope of the
social unit that is the State.

Chapter 2

Where does international law come from?

Where does international law comes from? There is a knot of related but distinct matters that are tied up in this question. Who says that a State must do this or that? Why do States obey the law? If rules of law are made by States in the first place, can they really be regarded as significant constraints upon States? This knot can usefully be unravelled at this stage.

The short and traditional answer to the question is that rules of international law come from two main sources, treaties and customary international law, both of which are created by States; and that States are, therefore, bound by the rules with which they have chosen to bind themselves—rules to which they have consented. This short, formalistic answer, however, gives little insight into what international law is really like or how it works.

The fact is that all around the world in government offices public officials routinely conduct their business within the framework of international law, and corporate officers and individuals, to the fast-increasing extent that they engage with international law, also do so. It is not so much a case of international law imposing constraints upon them: it is rather that the rules of international law largely spell out the normal way in which international transactions are conducted—the rules and principles that are tacitly accepted as the grammar of international bureaucracies, both public and private—so that in most cases it would require a conscious effort to act contrary to international law. Habit, torpor, and the pervasive desire of employees not to risk their careers and pensions by making the wrong decision: these are the main ingredients in the mixture that gives international law its great binding strength. What better answer to the question, 'why did you do that?' than to say 'that is how everyone always does it; and that is how the law says that we should do it'?

The ways in which this bureaucratic inertia operates become clearer when one considers the nature of customary international law and of treaties a little more closely.

Customary international law

Customary laws exist in many national legal systems, particularly in Africa and Asia, but also elsewhere. In English law, murder, for example, is not a crime created by statute, but a crime under common law, which developed as a customary law system.

Systems of customary law, including customary international law, are rooted in the regularity of an identified practice. Some rules of conduct become so ingrained in a society and are regarded as so important that a breach of them is regarded as particularly serious, attracting not merely social opprobrium but exposure to legal sanctions, including the sanctions of organized law enforcement—arrest, fining, imprisonment, and so on. For example, foreign heads of State and their diplomatic envoys have been recognized since time immemorial as having immunity from the jurisdiction of local courts. The practice of according such immunity is firmly established. It is followed by practically all States practically all of the time—the detention of the US diplomatic and consular staff in the US Embassy in Tehran in 1979 was a very rare exception, which was condemned as a violation of international law. The generality of the practice has established such immunity as a rule of customary international law, so that imprisoning an ambassador would be regarded not merely as an unfriendly and inhospitable act, but as an act which violated rights and obligations, and in response to which legal sanctions could be applied.

It is not necessary that every State subscribe to a practice in order for it to become a rule of customary international law: it is enough that a significant number of States do so, and particularly the major States and States especially affected by the rule (as the handful of States with the capacity to put rockets into space are the States specially affected by outer space law, for example). What matters above all is that there should be little or no disagreement with the putative rule—no significant divergent practice or opposition to the rule.

A metaphor that international lawyers often use to describe the emergence of rules of customary international law is that of the footpath. The metaphor has its limitations, but the central point is helpful. Regular following of the same track establishes an identifiable path, whether it be made by a few people or by many; and if there is an understanding that the path *should* be followed, it will be a clear path with little or no sign of people straying from it or trying to make new, competing paths. If, however, people wander all over the place so that there is no clear track, there can be no general expectation that people should conform to one particular route.

Regular practices that have the character of legal rules, such as the rules on diplomatic immunity, are distinguished from those practices that, while they may be equally consistently followed, are not strictly 'legal', such as the practice of remitting from time to time the intergovernmental debts of the very poorest countries. The important point is that in order to evidence a rule of customary international law the international practice must not simply be followed as a matter of fact, but must in addition be regarded as legally binding by the generality of States so that following the practice is not merely a matter of choice or policy but of legal obligation. The conviction that the rules are indeed legally binding, so that a State has the legal right (or duty, depending upon the content of the rule) to engage in the practice, and conversely so that States that act inconsistently with the practice are liable to face sanctions under international law, is known by the technical name of *opinio juris*.

We can tell which regular practices by States are considered to be governed by rules of international law by looking at what State officials say in relation to the practice. For instance, when WPC Yvonne Fletcher was fatally shot from a window in the Libyan People's Bureau in St James' Square, London, in 1984, the British government publicly took the position that as long as the building remained a diplomatic mission it enjoyed immunity and the police were not entitled to enter it. Government spokesmen explained that the practice was followed because of the international law on immunity—though the UK took swift action, in accordance with international practice, to terminate diplomatic relations with Libya and order the closure of the mission, after which (and having given the mission staff the opportunity to clear the premises and leave) its diplomatic immunity was lost. Those acts, coupled with the *opinio juris* in the form of the government's explanation of its actions, evidenced the UK's adherence to the rules on the immunity of diplomatic premises. Taken alongside similar evidence from other States, such episodes build up the picture of a 'general practice accepted as law' among States.

Searching for evidence of *opinio juris* by searching for clear statements of the views of governments is the hard way of identifying rules of customary international law. For the most part, there is general agreement on what those rules are, and the rules can be found set out in a systematic fashion in textbooks of international law.

It does not matter if the rule is often broken. Customary international law is rather like religion. If we were to ask what a particular religion requires of us, the authoritative answer would lie not in the actual practices of the current adherents of the religion, but in an exposition of orthodox theology, probably performed by a priest or theologian. We would look not to what believers actually do, but to what they, and the leaders of their community, say that they ought to do. Hypocrisy tends to have a bad reputation: but it has a vital role in maintaining moral standards. So does gossip. Hypocrisy and gossip permit the articulation of pure norms of behaviour, uncompromised by the often tiresome need to conform to them.

It does not matter how or why people begin to follow a particular rule. For example, the rules about the immunity from arrest of foreign sovereigns have their origins in beliefs that kings and emperors were divinely anointed, even if they were not actually divine themselves. Those rules proved useful in the conduct of relations between sovereigns (or at least they proved convenient, and no sovereign or government was inclined to give them up), and they continued to be followed when myths of divine kingship had long since given way to myths of authority rooted in the mandate of the people. The rules on sovereign immunity—now usually called State immunity, to reflect this political development and the fact that the immunity is enjoyed by a wide range of government officers and agents—remain a much-used part of international law.

If a rule of customary international law ceases to be useful, there will be pressure to change it. It used to be the case, for example, that English courts gave immunity to foreign States and their agencies in all contexts, including situations in which State-trading corporations in communist States were engaged in commercial transactions in the market place. There was much complaint that immunity in that context gave State trading companies an advantage not available to private companies; and in the *Trendtex* case in 1977 the English Court of Appeal, after reviewing the practice of courts in other countries, decided that the UK should come into line with continental States and apply a doctrine of 'restrictive immunity', where immunity is accorded in respect of 'governmental' but not 'commercial' acts. Parliament was preparing legislation which had the same effect, and which came into force the following year as the State Immunity Act. But international law is a part of English law and the English courts were entitled, and indeed bound, to apply international law as it stands from time to time, unless it is contrary to legislation.

Changes in customary international law are usually initiated by a single State or a small group of States unilaterally applying what they hope will become the new rule of international law. If enough other States acquiesce in the novel practice, and subsequently adopt the same position themselves by applying the new rule which the practice represents, the 'general practice' will soon cease to be that of following the old rule, and become that of following the new rule. Thus, in the 1940s and early 1950s a handful of South American States started to claim exclusive control over fish stocks within 200 miles of their coasts. Most other States at that time regarded those claims as unlawful, and insisted that coastal State rights over adjacent waters extended only for 3 or 12 miles (opinion among States was divided as to the precise distance; but there were no significant claims to more than 12 miles). Dissatisfaction with the narrowness of the geographical extent of coastal State rights, which left high seas fisheries free for plundering by factory fishing fleets from a handful of developed States, led many coastal States to reconsider their positions; and by the 1970s the practice of most States had fallen in behind the 200-milers. A new rule of customary international law had been made.

More recently, the use of force by ad hoc coalitions, in Kosovo, in Iraq, and in Libya, has raised the question whether a new rule of international law is emerging which permits the use of force in some circumstances in order to prevent massive human rights violations by incumbent governments. Episodes such as the NATO bombing in Kosovo in 1999, and the 'no-fly zone' imposed on Libya in 2011, are said by some to evidence the emergence of such a rule, although others see in them little more than a desire on the part of some western States to secure or to remove particular foreign regimes without becoming involved in ground wars. While the motive behind a new practice is not really relevant to the question of its adoption as a rule of customary international law, it can have a great effect upon the acceptance of the new practice by States in general. It is, however, important to recall that even if the western governments and press appear to be aligned behind particular developments, the view in other parts of the world may be very different.

Codification of customary international law

Sometimes the rules of customary international law are codified. The UN has an expert body, the International Law Commission ('ILC'), which reviews areas of the law and, where the customary law is sufficiently clear and is ripe for codification, adopts texts restating the law. Some of those texts may subsequently form the basis for discussions at international conferences at which the ILC text, modified by whatever amendments the participating States agree upon, may be adopted as treaties. The Vienna Convention on the Law of Treaties is one such treaty. Those treaties then become binding upon those States that choose to become parties to them. To the extent that the treaty accurately reflects customary international law, the underlying rules of customary law will bind all States, whether or not they choose to become parties to the treaty by ratifying them. The advantage in ratifying the treaty is that it brings to relations between the States Parties the certainty that comes from the ability to point to an explicit text which definitively sets out their rights and duties. Customary international law is, in its very nature, more difficult to identify and prove in cases where its content is disputed.

Sometimes the ILC texts are simply adopted as resolutions of the ILC and noted by the UN General Assembly. Even in that form they may prove very influential, being referred to by courts and tribunals, or by governments in diplomatic communications, as authoritative statements of customary international law. The leading example is the ILC's Articles on State Responsibility, adopted in 2001. Those Articles explain in general terms the circumstances in which States are held responsible for breaches of international law. They address matters such as the responsibility of States for the acts of their officials and institutions (including their legislatures, courts, administrations, and other governmental bodies); general defences to responsibility, such as the fact that a State acted (in limited and carefully defined circumstances) under coercion or *force majeure* or out of necessity; the consequences of responsibility, including the right of other States to take counter-measures in order to pressure the wrongdoing State back towards compliance with its obligations; and the right of injured States to reparation for injuries suffered. The rules of international law that are the subject of the breaches themselves are not set out in the ILC Articles: they are rules contained in treaties or in customary international law. The ILC Articles on State Responsibility have been immensely influential and are frequently cited in diplomatic exchanges and in national and international courts and tribunals.

The power of customary international law

Customary international law is enormously resilient. Most of its rules are observed by most States most of the time. As is, I hope, apparent, this is practically tautologous: States normally follow customary international law because customary international law consists of the practices that States normally follow (coupled with the conviction that the practices are expressions of rules of international law). Put another way, it is not so much a case of customary international law bestowing binding force upon certain rules of conduct, so making them into rules of international law.

Rather, customary international law *is* the body of rules of conduct that are regarded as legally binding.

That is not to say that customary international law has no constraining power, or—except in a very abstract sense—that States are free to choose what rules bind them. States make the rules when they are on their best behaviour, when they are asserting publicly the rules and standards which they believe must be observed. Often the statements are made when they are criticizing other States for not observing them. But existence of the rules exerts a real pull towards compliance when States are tempted to fall below the standards that they have themselves adopted; and that is a valuable source of normative pressure within the international system.

It is often not obvious to the outside world just how powerful this pressure is: but it is well known to those involved in the practice of international law, whether as government lawyers or ministers, or as corporate lawyers or as practitioners at the international Bar. It is far from uncommon for officials to say that a State will not put forward what would be a strong argument in defence of its actions, because that argument might be turned round and used against the State in future. Ideas of moral absolutes may have faded with the decline of religion and natural law, but the force of consistency as a moral imperative is largely undimmed (see Figure 3).

Only occasionally is the need for consistency challenged, as it has been in arguments of American 'exceptionalism'—the argument that because of its economic and military power the USA bears exceptional responsibilities within the international system, and that US interests should consequently be specially accommodated by the rules of international law. That argument, advanced most often in the context of the rules on the use of force and the claim that the USA is uniquely fitted for and uniquely burdened with the role of 'world policeman', has made little headway, however, and is unlikely to go much further. As other military and economic

3. Is consistency the highest moral value?

powers, such as the BRICS States—Brazil, Russia, India, China, and South Africa—and the EU, emerge at the global and regional level (and the changes in the notion of what is 'regional', as the reach of political, economic, and military power changes, is itself an important theme in international law), the days when any single State could claim to have special exemptions from the rules that bind the rest of the world are quickly passing. Every State has an interest in the consistency of rules, and in the predictability of behaviour for which such consistency is a precondition.

These points have been made in the context of a discussion of customary international law, but they apply equally to all legal rules, whatever their origin. Customary international law was the main source of international law until the middle of the 20th century; but it is now taking second place to treaties and other sources of law, to which I now turn.

Treaties

Customary law is resilient; but it can be slow and imprecise in the making. A practice must first be initiated. One must then wait for the pattern of State practice to become settled. Even when the practice is settled, it may not be comprehensive or exact. It may be clear that ambassadors are given immunity: but what of their children, or their spouses or partners? How much oil must be spilled into a State's waters before it counts as unlawful pollution? A bucketful? A barrel? Half a tanker load?

Then again, it may be that there is a need for rules in a field of activity in which concurrent State practices are unlikely to arise spontaneously—rules on international trade, tariffs, and subsidies are an example—or where there is a need for a new institution to be created—such as the International Criminal Court, the EU, or the UN—which cannot arise spontaneously from State practice. To take another set of problems, there may be circumstances where any one State will act only if it knows in advance what steps others will take: disarmament is an instance. In circumstances such as these, the obvious way, and often the only practical way, to proceed is by drawing up an express agreement, a treaty (see Figure 4).

One might speculate that the demise of the 19th-century system of Great Powers spelled the downfall of the informal consensus-based law-making that is exemplified by customary international law, and that the great increase in the number of independent State voices, coupled with the greatly increased possibilities for international travel and communication, made the deliberate negotiation of new rules of international law and their reduction to writing in treaties an almost inevitable development. Others might say that, in some contexts at least, the making of an international agreement is used as a substitute for action. General provisions in environmental and human rights treaties, exhorting the States Parties to implement the treaties to the fullest possible extent, are obvious examples: a vaguely worded catch-all treaty clause can often be slotted in when there is no possibility of reaching agreement on whatever it might mean. Yet again, one might say that customary international law had by the

4. States take treaties seriously. Kennedy signs the Nuclear Test Ban Treaty in 1963.

20th century done its work. It has laid out the basic framework of international relations, and the task is now to build on that framework with more detailed rules which can only be established through negotiation and the drafting of texts that command an explicit consensus. For whatever reason, treaties are now the most common means by which new rules of international law are made, as the ever more numerous volumes of the *United Nations Treaty Series*—currently around 2,600 volumes—show.

A treaty is simply an agreement between States that is legally binding. 'Treaty' is the generic name for legally binding agreements between States. Such agreements have a variety of titles, such as 'agreement', 'treaty', 'convention', 'pact', 'covenant', 'charter', 'protocol', and 'exchange of notes': the title of any particular instrument is little more than a matter of style and diplomatic tradition.

If States wish to set out their rights and duties in relation to one another in a clear and precise manner, they will usually do it by negotiating a bilateral or multilateral treaty. This has the advantage of precision and of speed, though complex multilateral treaties, such as the agreements constituting the World Trade Organization and the international trading system, can sometimes take many years to negotiate.

There is a balance to be struck in the context of multilateral treaty negotiations between the aims of maximizing participation by States and maximizing the extent of the commitments made by the Parties. Take, for instance, the 1979 UN Convention on the Elimination of Discrimination Against Women ('CEDAW'). In Article 2 of CEDAW the States Parties 'condemn discrimination against women in all its forms, [and] agree to pursue by all appropriate means and without delay a policy of eliminating discrimination against women'. The Convention proceeds to set out specific provisions by which the Parties are bound. But there are wide cultural differences in the ways in which women are regarded and treated. If the goal were that all States in the world should subscribe to CEDAW, the prohibitions on discrimination would have to be set at a level acceptable to the States most reluctant to commit themselves to the elimination of discrimination. If strength of commitment is the aim, the prohibitions could be set at the level that the States most willing to commit themselves would accept. (And, I should add, unwillingness to make international commitments is not the same as unwillingness to accept the underlying principles. Some States with very extensive legal guarantees in their national laws against sex discrimination may be reluctant to become Parties to treaties because of concerns that the obligations under the treaty do not mesh precisely with their domestic legislation. For instance, concerns about the implications of CEDAW for combat roles for women in military service, and for the provision of paid maternity leave, were raised in the USA as obstacles to US ratification of CEDAW, despite the clear acceptance of the desirability of eliminating discrimination based upon sex.)

One way of addressing the problem of securing the optimum balance between the breadth and depth of commitment by States to a given treaty is to permit States to make reservations to the treaty (or 'opt-outs', as they are commonly called in the EU context). A State making a reservation is saying, in essence, that it accepts the treaty with the exception of certain specific provisions, or subject to certain specific conditions set out in the reservation. For example, under CEDAW Australia made reservations concerning maternity leave, and India declared that 'though in principle it fully supports the principle of compulsory registration of marriages, it is not practical in a vast country like India with its variety of customs, religions and level of literacy'. Those are practical accommodations, necessary in order to enable Australia and India to accept the other obligations under CEDAW. Sometimes a reservation goes further. Saudi Arabia's reservation to CEDAW provides that 'in case of contradiction between any term of the Convention and norms of Islamic law, the Kingdom of Saudi Arabia is not under obligation to observe the contradictory terms of the Convention': thus can the shadow of a hand block out the sun.

Some treaties expressly permit certain reservations or forbid reservations to certain provisions in the treaty. If there is no such express provision, only reservations consistent with the object and purpose of the treaty may be made; and even then each other State Party can choose whether to accept the reservation (in which case the treaty applies between it and the reserving State as modified by the reservation), or to refuse to accept that the treaty comes into force at all between it and the reserving State, or to allow the treaty to enter into force but excluding the provisions to which the reservation relates, and on which it and the reserving State have, in effect, failed to agree.

These effects, like other matters concerning the making, validity, interpretation, and termination of treaties, are governed by legal principles set out in the 1969 Vienna Convention on the Law of

Treaties. That Convention was one of many that have been drafted by the ILC with a view to codifying customary international law or filling important gaps where evidence of customary international law was lacking or unclear.

Some treaties enter into force immediately; others, only after ratification, or sometimes only after ratification by a specified number of States regarded as the minimum necessary if the new treaty regime is to be viable and effective. In States such as the USA, where ratification requires the consent of the legislature, that can cause difficulties for the government, which negotiates treaties. The US Congress refused to give its consent to ratification of the Strategic Arms Limitation Treaty ('SALT II') negotiated by the Carter administration with the USSR in 1979; and Congressional opposition to the 1948 Havana Charter effectively blocked the first attempt to create a world trade organization—though the USA was one of the prime architects of the agreements that did eventually establish a World Trade Organization in 1994.

Some see internal opposition to treaties negotiated by a government as a sign of insularity and unwillingness to join in international attempts to grapple with global problems. Others see provisions such as the requirement for Congressional consent as an essential element in any democratic constitution. Why, after all, should it be possible for the government to decide on, say, tariff arrangements or military alliances with foreign States without recourse to parliament or its equivalent, when the imposition of a requirement to obtain a dog licence requires the active cooperation of the legislature and the pursuit of the full and ponderous procedures of law-making? Which affects the citizen more?

Such difficulties are avoided in different ways. In some States, prior consent is required for ratification of treaties; in others, such as the UK, the government has the right to enter into treaty commitments on its own authority and without any prior consent from the legislature. Conversely, however, there is a tendency (the exact position depends upon the constitutional law of each State) for those States that do require prior consent from the legislature to give treaties the force of law within the national legal system and before national courts, whereas States that do not require prior consent tend to deny treaties any such force unless they have been enacted into national law by legislation. Thus, while treaties made by the British government are legally binding upon the United Kingdom as a matter of international law, as a matter of English or Scots law and in English or Scottish courts a treaty is not applicable as a source of law unless it is has been implemented in English or Scots law by an Act of Parliament. The consequence is that the British government will not in practice ratify any treaty that requires some alteration in English law unless and until that alteration has already been obtained through parliamentary action. There is, therefore, some degree of democratic control on treaty-making, even under the British system.

Resolutions of the UN and other international organizations

In the discussion of Statehood, I referred to a number of UN General Assembly resolutions as though they were authoritative expositions of the law. Such references are regarded as rather louche by most international lawyers. Strictly speaking, resolutions of the UN and other international organizations cannot make international law. It is wrong, however, to regard them as having no legal significance whatever.

A resolution may affirm or restate established rules of international law, in which case the resolution might be cited as a convenient articulation of the rule. UN General Assembly resolution 2625 (XXV)—the great 1970 Declaration on Principles of International Law Concerning Friendly Relations and Cooperation Among States in Accordance with the Charter of the United Nations—is an example. It was negotiated long and hard within the UN, in an attempt during the Cold War years to set out the fundamental principles of international law that were accepted by all States as the basis for relations between them. As such, it is widely regarded as an authoritative restatement of customary international law.

A resolution may be an explanation by the institution of the way in which its Member States interpret provisions of the institution's constitutive charter. For example, UN General Assembly resolutions 1514 and 1541 are regarded as authoritative interpretations of provisions in the UN Charter concerning self-determination.

Sometimes organs of international organizations are given the power to take decisions that bind Member States. The EU has wider powers of this kind than any other organization; but on the international (rather than the regional) plane, the best-known example is the UN Security Council. It has the power to make binding determinations of the existence of a breach of or threat to international peace and security, and it may order States to take steps to address such situations. Such steps may include the severance of economic or travel links and other sanctions and, under Chapter VII of the Charter, a practically limitless range of measures, including the use of force, if it considers them necessary. The existence of a veto held by each of the five permanent members of the Security Council (China, France, Russia, UK, USA) has ensured that the power to order States to take action is used relatively sparingly. Russia and the USA are the two most frequent users of the veto; and the Israel/Palestine situation is the context in which vetoes have been used most frequently.

Other organizations have powers to take measures within the limits of their own competences. For example, the International Maritime Organization ('IMO') has the power to authorize traffic separation schemes in busy international waterways such as the Straits of Dover.

Those cases apart, resolutions of international organizations generally have little or no binding legal effect. They may express the views of the Member States (or at least of the necessary majority of Members) on particular questions, and those views may have considerable political force: but they would not in themselves change the legal position or bind Member States.

Other rules and standards

The main rules governing the conduct of international relations are to be found in customary international law and, increasingly, in treaties. But the main rules are not the whole story. The law may (and does) say that States have an obligation to prevent the pollution of the seas: but what does that mean? No massive offshore oil-rig blowouts, certainly: but what of the routine leakage of oil from ships in the ordinary course of navigation, or the washing out of empty oil tanks at sea? Is the discharge of 1,000 litres of oil into the waters of a port to be treated in the same way as the discharge of 1,000 litres of oil during the entire course of a round-the-world voyage? There comes a point where the implementation of broad principles set out in laws has to be mediated through detailed technical rules and standards.

This is less tedious than it might sound. The consequence of the need for such technical norms is that while government officials may negotiate the basic principles of a legal regime, the detailed measures of implementation are commonly either set by industrial, commercial, or scientific groups, or borrowed from them. A treaty may, for instance, require that a State apply 'best industry practice' to certain activities over which it has jurisdiction; and that best practice may be laid down in part by professional associations of engineers. The rules and standards need not be technical in the narrow sense. NGOs active in the fields of human rights and environmental protection have done a great deal to subtilize and stabilize the understanding of concepts such as 'torture' and 'toxic waste', and to counter the tendency of some governments and corporations to keep their activities within the law by redefining the crime.

In this way the process of international law-making is open to the influence of what is loosely called 'civil society'—roughly, any voluntary social group capable of articulating a collective opinion. Furthermore, such standards can easily be altered as technology and societal expectations develop: there is no need to negotiate entirely new treaties. There are scores of international organizations, governmental and non-governmental, which adopt and revise technical standards in this way, creating detailed rules and standards that give precise meaning to legal rules that are framed in more general terms, and which specify more exactly what is expected by way of compliance with those legal rules.

Where to find international law

All of these sources of international law are distilled into the summaries of the subject given in textbooks on the subject, such as the classic *Oppenheim's International Law* and the *Encyclopaedia of Public International Law* and their equivalents in other languages. More importantly, because the obligation of every State to comply with international law requires that State organs and agencies, such as the courts, the police and armed forces, public regulatory bodies, and the like, act in conformity with the State's obligations under international law, many States also publish accounts of international law as it is applicable within that State. Thus, *Halsbury's Laws of England* contains a volume on 'International Relations Law', which sets out the law on questions of international law that arise most commonly within the United Kingdom, such as the immunities of foreign States and diplomats, the permissible scope of a State's jurisdiction under international law, and the rights and duties of international organizations.

Much can be found on the internet. Many international organizations and non-governmental organizations have websites which not only set out the main legal instruments on particular topics, but also include detailed (if sometimes partisan) discussions of the law.

Chapter 3
Implementing international law

International law is implemented (a much more helpful notion than 'enforced') in many different ways. Most commonly, its rules are simply followed by State officials and others in their day-to-day routines. But sometimes the implementation is more formal and more noticeable.

Translating international law for national courts

The rules of international law are often given effect in municipal law by enacting them in statutes. For instance, in the UK the Diplomatic Privileges Act 1964 gives effect to the obligations of the UK in relation to diplomatic immunities, codified in the 1961 Vienna Convention on Diplomatic Relations; and the State Immunity Act 1978 gave effect to the rules on State immunity as the UK understood them to exist in customary international law, before those rules were codified in the 2004 UN Convention on Jurisdictional Immunities of States.

In the UK rules of customary international law may be applied directly by the courts, but rights and obligations created by treaty can be applied only if they are incorporated by means of legislation into domestic law. In the USA, in contrast, not only may the courts apply rules of customary international law, but the Constitution gives to treaties ratified by Congress a status equivalent to legislation. Whether legislation is necessary to implement customary international law or treaties within a national legal system is, as has already been noted, a matter for the constitutional law of each State. Where legislation is required, the courts will look to the domestic statute, rather than to international law: even some of those participating in a trial may be unaware of the underlying international law that finds expression in the applicable statutes.

It is sometimes suggested that the world would be a better place if all national courts applied international law, and gave it precedence over inconsistent national law. The expectation is that activities such as governmental action in breach of human rights laws, or the conduct of wars in breach of international law, or trade in breach of UN sanctions, could all be struck down by national courts to which, unlike most international courts, individuals would have direct access. But that is not necessarily desirable.

All political structures are built on the human scale. Parliamentary gatherings are of a size, and sessions are of a length, that makes effective communication possible. Governmental structures devolve responsibilities to levels where effective political action and control can be sustained. And, at least in States that maintain some pretension to democracy, political responsibility is secured through an institutionalized relationship that makes dialogue between the electorate and their representatives feasible. So, if people consider that a particular law should be changed, they can bring pressure to bear and the legislature can take appropriate action. People have a measure of control over the laws that the courts apply; and those laws can be tailored to fit the traditions and the situations in each individual State. That kind of political control cannot be made effective at a global level. There is no possibility of citizens having real control over the making of customary international law or of treaties. The direct and automatic application of all rules of international law in national courts is not something that fits together easily with democratic systems of government within individual States.

Sight must not be lost of the fact that international conferences and international organizations are, at heart, no more than gatherings of national governmental officials and their agents and employees. The roles of the international policy-makers may be global, but their lives and careers (with the possible exception of the international civil servants who form the permanent backbones of these organizations) are local, rooted in their home States. They are no more immune from the risk of taking bad decisions in the UN than they are from the risk of taking bad decisions within national governments; and they are no less in need of a system of courts to maintain the Rule of Law. But the impracticability of global structures of political responsibility means that a system of effective judicial review cannot be located at the international level. Better to be able to fight bad policies within national courts, using arguments drawn from international law even if it does not automatically prevail over national law, than to address pleas and petitions to the post-boxes of international organizations. All real political battles are ultimately local.

Compliance and remonstration

What happens if a State breaks a rule of international law? The first point to make is that it is often not entirely certain when a State has broken the law. States are in fact remarkably consistent in conducting themselves in accordance with the established rules, just as individuals generally conduct themselves in accordance with national laws. In the same way that people will voluntarily form and maintain queues, even in the absence of any legal obligation or coercion, States tend to comply with international law. But even where a State does appear to have violated international law, it is often the case that it considers itself to have acted within its rights, and that the immediate dispute concerns

41

what international law requires rather than whether the requirements have been met. The invasion of Iraq by the UK and the USA in 2003 was widely regarded as incompatible with international law; but there is little doubt that many in the governments of those two States were (or allowed themselves to become) convinced that a legal justification for the invasion could be made out.

The second point to make is that the great majority of international differences are sorted out by talking. Multilateral discussions in organizations such as the UN and the IMF; bilateral negotiations between the disputing States; sequences of unilateral speeches, and press releases that clarify the States' intentions and understandings: all serve to make clear the position of a State that is regarded as being in breach of its international obligations and thus to enable others to decide if any further action is needed. If action is indeed needed, States have a wide range of tools at their disposal.

It is widely supposed that in contrast to systems of municipal law, where wrongdoers are pursued by the police and brought to trial and punished, in international law very little happens if a State chooses not to fulfil its legal obligations. That view is misconceived. Municipal law is not systematically enforced. In the case of criminal law, most estimates suggest that fewer than half of the crimes committed are reported to the police; and of those reported, a suspect is identified only in a minority of cases. More importantly, a wide variety of violations of the criminal law, including domestic violence, so-called 'victimless crimes' such as drug offences, road traffic offences, and a good deal of petty theft from shops and employers, are not treated as crimes at all, so that they do not even show up in statistics of 'unreported' crimes. And all of this focuses only upon the criminal law. The number of violations of legal obligations that would result if civil wrongs such as trespass, defamation, breaches of contract, and negligence were added to the list, is incalculably high.

It is not intended that every violation of the law should be prosecuted. There are more important priorities on which to spend public money. It is enough that the law is available to be used when necessary, to try to prevent violations from reaching unacceptable levels in particular communities, and to prevent perpetrators of high-profile offences from escaping with impunity. Indeed, even when criminal charges are brought, it is increasingly common to prescribe some remedial sentence, such as attendance at a 'speeding awareness' course, instead of a penalty.

International law is no different. There is neither the expectation nor the intention that international law should be enforced on every occasion when it is violated. Many minor violations are willingly tolerated as the products of human frailty, or as not worth pursuing. An accidental trespass a few metres over an international border by armed forces in a remote forested area, or a minor breach of World Trade Organization rules on subsidies to domestic producers, will probably be overlooked because they are the kinds of breach that cause no substantial harm and do not call the basic rules into question. If a breach is regarded as provocative, as in the case of the deliberate overflight of disputed territory by military aircraft for instance, a diplomatic protest may be made. The nuances of international diplomacy, outlined in volumes such as *Satow's Diplomatic Practice*, are so well understood that the choices of language, form, author, and recipient of diplomatic communications enable States to signal with considerable precision the degree of outrage or criticism behind the protest.

Protests are by no means insignificant, because disapproval and a cooling of relations between States is not insignificant. There are many ways in which States can make life easier for other States and their nationals even though they are not legally obliged to do so. The amendment of visa requirements, including the difficulty and cost of procedures for obtaining visas; awards of government contracts; the grant or withholding of overflight rights for aircraft: the range of possible measures is enormous, and the cost to the target State of the imposition of such measures can be very high indeed. The imposition of unfriendly measures and the removal of friendly concessions are known as acts of 'retorsion' when they involve no breach of any legal obligation. But States may go further.

One of the principles of international law is that where a State is injured by an unlawful act of another State it is entitled to suspend its own performance of some obligation owed to the wrongdoing State, in order to induce the wrongdoer to come back into line with its obligations. Such suspensions of the performance of legal obligations are known as counter-measures. They are, by definition, in one sense themselves breaches of international law (which measures of retorsion are not); but they are justified and rendered lawful by the prior illegal act of the State against which the counter-measures are taken, and are therefore lawful. Counter-measures must be proportionate to the wrong suffered, and must not violate the rules of international law on the protection of human rights and on the use of force. They might include prohibitions on the performance of contracts and other commercial dealings with the target State, for example; and sometimes they are organized as full 'sanctions regimes', deliberately designed to apply pressure to the target State to force it to change its ways.

Sanctions are not always directed against States. Individuals and corporations suspected of association with international terrorist groups have also been targeted. Those 'Al Qaida and Taliban' sanctions, imposed under a series of UN Security Council resolutions, beginning with resolution 1267 (1999), have attracted some criticism. Individuals are put on to a list by a UN Security Council sanctions committee, on the basis of reports from UN Member States of which only the sketchiest summaries are made available to the people affected, and which may rely heavily upon untested allegations. Once listed, States are obliged to apply the sanctions to the listed people. The affected individuals cannot challenge the sanctions in the UN itself, but may challenge them in the domestic courts of the States that apply them; but there is a strong tendency for national governments and courts to hide behind the authority of the UN and to say that they have no choice but to apply the sanctions. It is an illuminating instance of the problems that can arise from the relationship between international law and municipal law.

Sometimes disputes are serious and intractable and cannot be settled by discussion and the application of indications of discontent and disapproval. States then have a choice as to how they deal with them, just as individuals do in respect of their own disputes. A dispute over a neighbour's garden hedge or loud parties may be taken off to court, or it may be allowed to simmer, with occasional acts of retorsion such as the nocturnal use of electric lawn-mowers, in the hope that the neighbour will in time become more reasonable. There is a legal route, and a non-legal route; and the offended individual will decide which is likely to be more effective and affordable.

So it is with States. In 1979, during the Islamic revolution in Iran, militant students kept US diplomats and their families hostage for many months in the US Embassy compound in Tehran. After an aborted attempt at a military rescue the United States took the matter to the International Court of Justice ('ICJ'). That move resulted in a judgment clearly upholding the rights of the US nationals. Coupled with measures of retorsion in the form of a dramatic decline in bilateral US–Iran trade, and the imposition by the USA of a freeze on $12 billion of Iranian assets held in US banks as a counter-measure, the ICJ judgment paved the way for a solution to the dispute, mediated by Algeria and involving the establishment of an international tribunal—the Iran–USA Claims Tribunal, which is still sitting in The Hague—to hear and settle claims by nationals of one State against the government of the other, as well as claims between the two States. The settlement process involved many components: an unsuccessful attempt at self-help, retorsion, counter-measures, litigation, arbitration, mediation. The episode illustrates the range of steps available to States for the handling of international law disputes.

State responsibility

The traditional inter-State model of international law places States in the role of defenders of their nationals. In the words of the Permanent Court of International Justice (the predecessor of the ICJ), in the *Mavrommatis* case,

> It is an elementary principle of international law that a State is entitled to protect its subjects, when injured by acts contrary to international law committed by another State, from whom they have been unable to obtain satisfaction through the ordinary channels. By taking up the case of one of its subjects and by resorting to diplomatic action or international judicial proceedings on his behalf, a State is in reality asserting its own rights—its right to ensure, in the person of its subjects, respect for the rules of international law.

There is a symmetry here. Just as States may defend the rights of their nationals (be they individual human beings or legal persons such as companies) because an injury done to a national in breach of international law may amount to a wrong done *to* the national State, so too an action of an individual or corporation may amount to an action *of* a State. The attribution of acts to States is the concern of the doctrine of State responsibility.

Acts of individuals or corporations are attributable to a State when those acts are exercises of the legislative, executive, judicial, or other 'governmental' functions of that State. Each State has the right to choose its own governmental structures as an aspect of the principles of sovereignty and self-determination, and so all levels and designations of national, regional, or provincial and local government are regarded as parts of the government of the State.

All acts of the government are obviously 'State' acts, but acts of private individuals are, in principle, not. So, for example, if I am assaulted by a policeman or immigration official in a State, that State is responsible for that action; but if the assault is committed by a private citizen (say, a rioting football supporter) the State is not responsible for the assault—though if the State had foreknowledge of the riot and failed to take reasonable steps to protect persons and property known to be at particular risk, the State might be internationally responsible for that failure.

The responsibility of a State for acts of 'governmental' bodies is usually quite clear. But there are difficult cases. Acts of the regular police are plainly attributable to the State, but what about private security guards employed to guard prisoners or public transport facilities or private banks? National courts are plainly State organs, but what about professional disciplinary bodies, or religious courts, that operate within the State? Are the questions whether the postman or a doctor is employed by the State or by a private company, or whether an oil company is owned in whole or in part by the State, relevant to the question of the attribution of their conduct to the State? Questions such as these are addressed by the rules of customary international law which, as was noted, were restated by the ILC in its 2001 Articles on State Responsibility.

Deciding disputes in international law

The settlement of international disputes begins with discussions, often conducted through the Foreign Ministries or diplomatic missions of the States concerned, but sometimes through other appropriate government ministries or agencies. Discussion may settle the dispute; but in any event it is only through discussion that it can be determined what, precisely, is in dispute.

Municipal courts

If discussion fails to resolve the dispute the matter may be sent to a court for decision. Often the first reference will be to a national court. For example, the extradition of General Pinochet from London to Spain was sought in respect of crimes that he was alleged to have committed while he was the Head of State in Chile. The question arose whether he was entitled to immunity as a former Head of State. That question was tried in the British courts, with the case making its way from the metropolitan stipendiary magistrate from whom the arrest warrant was first sought, through the Court of Appeal to the House of Lords. Those courts saw a full and detailed discussion of the international law on the immunities of Heads of State. Though the courts' final decision was that Pinochet did not enjoy immunity in respect of some of the offences with which he was charged, he was eventually released on medical grounds by the Home Secretary. Had Spain or Chile wished to dispute the decision of the courts or of the Home Secretary, the matter could in principle have been taken further, to an international court or tribunal.

International courts and tribunals

I say 'in principle' because, unlike national courts, international courts have no compulsory jurisdiction. A State is only obliged to appear before an international court or tribunal if it has consented to be subject to its jurisdiction.

That restriction is a very substantial constraint upon the jurisdiction of international courts and tribunals; but it should not be overstated. States can, and do, submit to the jurisdiction of international courts in various ways. Thus, under the Statute of the ICJ a State may sign up to accept the jurisdiction of the Court in respect of any legal dispute that another State making a similar declaration may bring against it. Fewer than one-third of States have done that, and many of them have attached exceptions ('reservations') to their acceptances. It is more common for States to accept the jurisdiction of the ICJ by adhering to treaties which include clauses which entitle each State Party to refer disputes with another Party arising from the treaty to refer the matter to an international court or tribunal. The 1948 Genocide Convention, for example, which has 146 Parties, provides that any Party may submit any dispute relating to the interpretation, application, or fulfilment of the Convention, including questions of the responsibility of a State for genocide, to the ICJ.

The ICJ is technically the principal judicial organ of the United Nations, as the Permanent Court of International Justice ('PCIJ') was in relation to the League of Nations. The PCIJ and ICJ are sometimes referred to collectively as the 'International Court' or the 'World Court'. The International Court sits in the Peace Palace in The Hague (see Figure 5), which was built before the League of Nations was established, and was intended to accommodate the ad hoc arbitration tribunals for which the 1899 Hague Convention on the Pacific Settlement of Disputes provided. The Permanent Court of Arbitration, which was established by the 1899 Convention and which organizes many such arbitrations, still has

5. The Peace Palace in The Hague. The resemblance to Disneyland is accidental.

its seat in the Peace Palace. The International Court is not the oldest judicial forum.

Nor does the ICJ have any formal authority over other tribunals. Though some self-contained dispute settlement systems, such as that which forms a part of the World Trade Organization ('WTO'), have their own appeal chambers, there is no general hierarchy of international tribunals or system of appeals in international law, although in practice most other tribunals show considerable deference to rulings of the International Court. Nor does the International Court hear the majority of international law cases. In fact, only a very small proportion of the cases that are decided by the application of rules of international law are taken to the International Court.

The latter point is particularly important. Most cases in which international law is applied arise in municipal courts and tribunals. Cases concerning applications for asylum and refugee status are a sadly common example: it is the Asylum and Immigration Tribunals which are primarily responsible for adjudicating upon the fulfilment of the legal obligations which the UK, along with 144 other States, undertook by ratifying the 1951 Convention relating to the Status of Refugees (and it is an interesting and instructive way of whiling away an hour or so to look on the internet to see which States have *not* ratified this and other treaties that safeguard elementary human rights). International law is often at work under the surface of national laws in national courts.

There are, moreover, many international courts and tribunals; and their number is growing. Almost all of them have a limited and specialized jurisdiction, confined to matters such as human rights (the European, Inter-American and African Courts of Human Rights), economic and trade matters (the courts of the regional economic communities such as the Andean Community, the Caribbean Community (CARICOM), the European Union, the

Mercado Común del Sur (MERCOSUR), and the Southern African Development Community (SADC), for example), the law of the sea (the International Tribunal for the Law of the Sea (ITLOS)), criminal law (the International Criminal Court (ICC) and the ad hoc tribunals established to deal with war crimes and crimes against humanity in the Former Yugoslavia, Rwanda, Sierra Leone, and Cambodia, for example), sport (the Court of Arbitration for Sport), and intellectual property (the arbitral tribunals organized by the World Intellectual Property Organization (WIPO)). In addition, there are many arbitration tribunals established by agreement on a case-by-case basis in order to decide international disputes.

These specialized tribunals handle far more cases than the ICJ. For example, in 2013, the European Court of Human Rights ('ECtHR') received almost 66,000 applications: it disposed of over 93,000 cases, the vast majority of which were declared to be inadmissible, but still had a backlog of around 100,000 pending applications in 2014 (more than half of them against Russia, Italy, Ukraine, or Serbia). The dispute settlement mechanism of the WTO has been invoked in almost 500 cases since its establishment in 1995, in relation to matters such as agricultural subsidies, restrictions on trade in beef from hormone-treated cattle, and China's exports of footwear.

International tribunals can be divided into two broad categories, depending upon the way in which they relate to States and individuals. Both the ECtHR and the WTO—to take a prominent example of each category—handle cases of direct significance for individuals, but they do so in rather different ways. The ECtHR in Strasbourg handles cases brought by individuals who have been unable to find a legal remedy within the national courts of the State Party to the European Convention on Human Rights against which they complain. The individuals initiate ECtHR proceedings in their own names and they control the litigation, deciding for example whether to press ahead or to settle or abandon the case.

The individuals seek the vindication of rights protected by the Convention, such as the right to a fair trial and the right to freedom of expression.

In the WTO system, on the other hand, cases may be brought only by, and against, States (and the EU, which exercises the rights of its Member States in WTO trade matters). It was the USA, for example, and not US farmers, which brought the complaint against the EU restrictions on imports of meat containing artificial hormones. But the underlying structure of the disputes in the ECtHR and the WTO is not very different. The USA was responding to pressure upon its government by its farmers, and the US government was protecting their interests through the WTO. Although the farmers had no individual right to export beef to the EU, the practical result of the WTO procedures was essentially the same as that which would have followed a procedure in which the farmers were asserting their own rights.

The ECtHR is one example, along with human rights tribunals in other parts of the world, and with the hundreds of ad hoc tribunals set up under bilateral investment treaties to adjudicate upon disputes between investors and host States, and with the Iran–USA Claims Tribunal, of a 'mixed tribunal' or 'State/non-State tribunal'—that is, a tribunal in which individuals or corporations have the right to institute and appear as parties in cases against States, calling the State to account for its actions, though only within the scope of the tribunal's jurisdiction, and on a footing of equality with the respondent State. The WTO dispute settlement procedure, on the other hand, like the ICJ, is an inter-State body: individuals and corporations have no right to invoke the procedure, and they cannot be made defendants in that procedure.

Though there were earlier formalized proceedings for the settlement of international disputes, such as those set up under the 1794 Jay Treaty to settle disputes between the USA and Britain concerning debts and boundaries that had arisen during the American War of Independence, the modern tradition of international courts is usually said to have begun with the tribunal established in Geneva to settle the *Alabama* claims. Those were claims for compensation made by the USA against Britain for damage caused during the American Civil War to Union shipping by the Confederate warship the *CSS Alabama*, built in Birkenhead and supplied to the Confederacy in breach of Britain's obligations under international law as a neutral in the War. The *Alabama* captured or sank sixty-five merchant ships trading with the Union, before it was sunk off Cherbourg in 1864.

The most prominent international courts and tribunals established in the century after the *Alabama* claims were inter-State bodies. Cases in which an individual or corporation suffered loss as a result of a breach of international law for which a foreign State was responsible were taken up by the national State of the injured person, in negotiations or before an international tribunal. The more recent trend in the establishment of international tribunals, however, is towards the mixed tribunal model. There are several reasons for this.

First, there is the reluctance of governments to devote scarce public resources to the vindication of the particular rights of an individual or corporation, and to complicate its relations with the respondent State by litigating against it.

Second, as the range of matters regulated by international agreement expands, particularly into areas touching upon commercial and industrial activity, rules of international law have increasingly been addressed directly to the rights and duties of individuals and corporations, rather than States. For instance, States have long been obliged to treat foreign corporations with at least a minimum standard of fairness; but since the 1960s hundreds of bilateral investment treaties ('BITs') have been concluded by States which give foreign investors rights to fair and equitable treatment, to non-discrimination, not to have their property expropriated, and so on; and under most of these BITs the investors themselves have the right to institute proceedings against the host State before international arbitration tribunals if they consider that their rights have been violated.

In order to make this shift from an inter-State to a mixed model work, it is necessary for host States to ensure that their national laws do in fact secure the rights that are granted under the BITs, and for corporate officers and their advisers to become aware of the investor's rights under the BIT. Mixed tribunals thus go hand in hand with what might be called the domestication or internalization of international law—the view that rules and principles of international law are not simply matters of concern to governments, but are of direct and immediate relevance to the decisions and acts of private individuals and corporations. Hence the current importance of regional human rights courts, international investment tribunals, and (on a somewhat different plane, because of the claim of the European Community and European Union that EU law is a legal order distinct from and, within its sphere of operation, superior to, both national and international law) the European Court of Justice.

Individuals are also very obviously engaged by international law in the various international criminal tribunals. The ad hoc international tribunals for the former Yugoslavia and for Rwanda, established by the UN Security Council, revived the vision of legal accountability for those accused of war crimes and crimes against humanity. That vision stood in contrast to the risk of the crimes being committed with impunity, as such people retired (often with a hefty slice of the wealth of their country) to an accommodating foreign State; and it strove to make clear that such tribunals were not instances of 'victor's justice', as some had alleged of the war crimes tribunals established in Nuremberg and Tokyo after the Second World War.

The war crimes tribunals established following the Second World War were the crucial step in ending the paradox that those politicians and military men with the greatest power and responsibility for the direction of war crimes escaped trial, let alone sanctions, for their crimes. But punishment was only a part of their function. Arguably even more important was their role in painstakingly uncovering and recording the truth. Confronting the past remains an important element in the decision to refer cases to international criminal tribunals.

The ad hoc international criminal tribunals were augmented by the International Criminal Court ('ICC'), established under the 1998 Rome Statute. The ICC has a complementary jurisdiction, prosecuting persons alleged to have committed a listed war crime or crime against humanity within the territory or by a national of a State Party to the Rome Statute but only if the alleged offence is not being genuinely pursued by national criminal authorities. There are also hybrid tribunals, such as the Special Court for Sierra Leone and the Extraordinary Chambers in the Courts of Cambodia, which introduce an international element into what are essentially domestic courts, in order to provide some international oversight and objectivity in the trial of serious and acutely political crimes.

Despite this increasing engagement between international law and individuals, however, the particular focus of international law remains fixed upon States. Chapters 4–7 explore some of the ways in which the principles of international law define the structure of international relations.

Chapter 4
Freedom from external interference

There are two things that people tend to expect from the law: that it keeps other people off their backs and leaves them free to organize their lives as they choose, and that it climbs onto other peoples backs so as to oblige them to do things for the common good. These functions, which are not mutually exclusive, correspond to two ways in which States come together to achieve common goals: by decentralized, ad hoc arrangements to meet particular needs, and by the creation of pre-planned systems and processes in which States are organized for the pursuit of agreed aims.

International law supports both approaches. Chapters 4 and 5 consider the ways in which international law underpins and secures the freedom of States; and Chapters 6 and 7 consider the attempts made to organize areas of international activity by using the mechanisms of international law.

This is far from being the only way that international law can be examined. Accounts of international law could be written that emphasize the ways in which its principles have operated to support colonialism and the commercial imperialism that has succeeded it, or the ways in which its principles are largely derived from Eurocentric legal and political concepts, or the ways in which its principles reflect the preoccupations of male-dominated societies or of western class structures. I make no claim that the perspective adopted here is more insightful (let alone more truthful or accurate) than any other. The best perspective depends upon what you want to see; and I have assumed that most readers will want to increase their understanding of international law in a way that meshes with what they hear and read about it in the English-language news media and in books written by scholars working in adjacent disciplines such as international relations. The preoccupations in the media are with the role of law in the control of international violence and in securing cooperation to address what are regarded as the major international problems of the day.

With the warning that this text has, in the language of theatre box offices, a restricted view, I move on in this chapter to examine one aspect of the assurance of the sovereign equality and independence of States and the freedom that it entails for each of them: the freedom from external interference, and in particular the freedom from forcible coercion by other States.

The prohibition on the use of force in international relations

The concept of freedom from external coercion has been a persistent theme of international law. It was particularly prominent in the writings of international lawyers such as Grigory Tunkin, schooled in Soviet theories of international law, for whom peaceful coexistence between States was the fundamental value and aim of the international legal system. The legal duty of foreign States not to interfere in the affairs of other States was a useful reinforcement of more positive formulations of the supremacy of the will of the people: both supported the view that each State must be left free to pursue its own chosen goals. If global revolution was not a realistic objective, at least the revolutions in individual countries could be protected; and for non-revolutionary States, there was the prospect of being left to their reactionary ways. So the theory went; and it was one of the axioms that supported the peace during the Cold War.

The basic concept that States have a right to go about their business in peace, free from intervention and coercion by other States, remains central to international law even though the principle of peaceful coexistence is now rarely referred to by name. One of the clearest principles of contemporary international law is that States are not free to threaten or use military force against each other or to intervene in each other's affairs. That is one reason why, for example, western States have been ready to take action against terrorist groups in Iraq, where the States act at the invitation of the Iraqi government, but have been very reluctant to take such action in Syria, where there is no such invitation.

The view that the right of nations to use force against each other is constrained by at least some rules of conduct is ancient, and it extends across many, perhaps all, cultures. Indeed, reference to the *right* to use force in international relations, rather than to the *fact* of the use of force, carries the necessary implication that the use of force is constrained by rules. Three sets of issues arise: in what circumstances may force be used? what weapons and methods of waging war may be used? and who is entitled to use force?

The rules of international law relating to war are traditionally divided into two parts: the *jus in bello* (also called international humanitarian law, or 'the laws of war'), which governs matters such as prohibitions on certain weapons and ways of waging war against other nations, and the *jus ad bellum*, which limits the circumstances in which there is a right to use even lawful methods of waging war—that is, limitations on the right to go to war at all.

Fighting within the rules: the *jus in bello*

The earliest rules relating to the use of force focused on the limitations upon the ways in which a war may properly be fought. The use of gratuitous violence which serves no military purpose or which causes unnecessary suffering is depraved, and it is natural that it should be forbidden as a matter of fundamental morality, even in circumstances where there are no clearly established rules as to when force may be used at all.

Prohibitions on certain ways of fighting are found in the most ancient legal texts. The use of poisoned weapons and the killing of people who have surrendered was prohibited by the *Dharmasastra* texts in India more than 2,000 years ago, for instance; and similar rules appear in the Deuteronomic code in the Bible. There have long been explicit agreements between States limiting the kinds of force that can properly be used: the 1868 Declaration of St Petersburg, under which the Parties renounced the use of small explosive shells that injured rather than killed and were thought to cause unnecessary suffering, is one example. This tradition of outlawing certain weapons and methods of warfare continues to the present day, with bans on biological and chemical weapons and anti-personnel landmines reflecting the response of the international community to the more recent creations of those whose contribution to human well-being consists in the invention of increasingly profligate ways of maiming and killing.

It is sometimes thought bizarre that the law should outlaw some weapons, such as poison gas, but give what appears to be approval to other means of killing. For someone who is committed to absolute pacifism, that position is indeed unreasonable. But for the majority of people, who are willing to accept the use of potentially lethal force to protect important interests or values in at least some circumstances, it is no more odd than permitting the police to question suspects while prohibiting them from using torture. The rules of the *jus in bello* are an essential acknowledgement that we share a common humanity with our enemies. Although we may ultimately be prepared to kill in order to prevent them doing certain things, we are nonetheless killing fellow human beings; and whatever the rightness of our cause, the use of unnecessary violence can never be justified. The weight of that observation is rarely felt more keenly than it is by the military officers whose job it is to decide whether particular proposed uses of force are justifiable.

The International Committee of the Red Cross ('ICRC') was established in 1863 by Henri Dunant (a somewhat controversial Swiss businessman, later awarded the first Nobel Peace Prize for his humanitarian work) and four of his colleagues, and has been pressing the cause of humanitarian law ever since. The ICRC, which was itself awarded the Nobel Peace Prize in 1917, has promoted many efforts to set out and to secure the implementation of rules limiting the barbarity of war, beginning with the 1864 Geneva Convention for the Amelioration of the Condition of the Wounded and Sick in Armed Forces in the Field, and continuing through to the current (1949) versions of the Geneva Conventions and the Protocols that supplemented them.

There are many generally accepted limitations on the weapons and tactics that may be used in wartime. Many of them are set out in the four Geneva Conventions of 1949, and the two Additional Protocols of 1977 which deal respectively with international armed conflicts and with non-international (internal) armed conflicts. (A third protocol, adopted in 2005, adopted the 'red crystal' as an international symbol to indicate protected persons and objects, alongside the red cross and red crescent symbols.) The Geneva Conventions also prescribe rules on matters such as the treatment of prisoners of war, and on the rights and duties of States that are in occupation of foreign territory. The latter rules, along with rules from the 1907 Hague Convention on the Laws and Customs of War on Land, are applicable to the Israeli occupation of the Occupied Palestinian Territory in the West Bank and Gaza, for example.

On some questions of humanitarian law, States disagree. For example, some States oppose moves to ban cluster munitions—shells that burst open to release many small bomblets, designed to kill people or destroy military matériel. These munitions, along with land mines, are a major cause of post-conflict injury and death, because armies rarely clean up completely what are called (in the language of Protocol V to the 1980 Convention on Certain Conventional Weapons) the 'explosive remnants of war'. They are left lying around, and may be picked up or accidentally detonated by children or other civilians. The risks associated with the use of such munitions is horribly evident; but to support a complete ban on them would require a State to decide that their use could never be justified, no matter how desperate the military situation or how sincere the commitment to clean up the battlefield after the conflict. One can see the reasoning of the States that oppose outright bans, even if one does not accept it; and they are, of course, the States most likely to use such weapons.

The most notorious difference of opinion on international humanitarian law between States concerns the treatment of persons said to be implicated in what the administration of US President George Bush labelled 'the War on Terror'—a term that owes more to public relations thinking than it does to the law. Many such persons, not members of any regular army, were categorized as 'unlawful combatants' and detained without trial in the detention facility operated by the United States in Guantanamo Bay, on territory leased by the USA from Cuba. Many of them were not even charged with having committed any criminal offence—let alone convicted of any such offence. They were denied both the protections afforded by the Geneva Conventions to members of regular armed forces acting in accordance with the laws of war, and also the protections that US domestic law would give to persons prosecuted under the normal criminal law for murder and other offences. The mistreatment of detainees, through their detention without charge and by subjecting them to 'enhanced interrogation techniques' such as water-boarding (which were examined in detail in the US Senate report on the CIA's Detention and Interrogation programme and use of various forms of torture), aroused great public concern and seriously tarnished the reputation of the United States and the other States that colluded with it, justifying their actions by the need to act to protect freedom in western States.

Progress on the reduction of unnecessary suffering in armed conflict is slow and piecemeal; and on some questions there is no international consensus. There are, however, four basic principles firmly accepted by all. These are the principles of (1) *military necessity* (which permits the use of only that degree and kind of force, not otherwise prohibited by the law of armed conflict, that is required to achieve the legitimate military purpose of the conflict); (2) *distinction* (which requires discrimination between the armed forces and military targets and, on the other hand, non-combatants, civilians, and civilian targets); (3) *proportionality* (which requires that losses resulting from a military action should not be excessive in relation to the military advantage expected to be gained from the action); and, above all, (4) *humanity* (which forbids the infliction of suffering, injury, or destruction not necessary for the accomplishment of legitimate military purposes).

The implications of these principles, and of more detailed prohibitions on weapons and tactics, are spelled out in military manuals issued by many States, such as *The Manual of the Law of Armed Conflict* issued by the UK Ministry of Defence in 2004.

Serious violations of the laws of war, such as the deliberate targeting of civilian non-combatants or the wanton destruction of towns and villages, amount to war crimes, for which the perpetrators may be punished by national courts, or by an international criminal tribunal that has jurisdiction over the events in question. Such international tribunals have been established on an ad hoc basis following the conflicts in the former Yugoslavia and in Rwanda, and (in slightly different hybrid forms, as 'internationalized criminal courts'—national courts with some international judges) for Cambodia, East Timor, Kosovo, and

Sierra Leone. There is also the permanent International Criminal Court ('ICC') established in 2002 under the 1998 treaty known as the Rome Statute. By the end of 2013 the ICC had exercised its jurisdiction in relation to seven conflicts, all of them in Africa, and was investigating alleged war crimes and crimes against humanity in other situations.

The most significant aspect of these tribunals is not simply that they continue the practice of prosecuting war crimes, but rather that the tribunals follow the lead of the war crimes trials after the Second World War, prosecuting those at the highest levels of government, and not only the military personnel who carry out their instructions.

Fighting on the right occasions: the just war

The development of the *jus in bello* throughout modern history has been essentially in one direction: towards the increasingly strict limitation of permissible weapons and methods of war to those which serve the four key principles—military necessity, distinction, proportionality, and humanity. The development of the *jus ad bellum*, on the other hand, has a less clear trajectory. For most of the 20th century the trend was towards the limitation of the circumstances in which war could properly be used as an instrument of foreign policy. But in the past decade or so there have been clear signs of a partial reversal of that trend. Nonetheless, the basic view that armed force may be used against other States only in very limited circumstances remains unchallenged.

The 'Just War' doctrine, refined by Thomas Aquinas, writing within the Judaeo-Christian tradition, is among the best-known articulations in the English-speaking world of what became the *jus ad bellum*; but it is by no means the only or the oldest such tradition. For example, over a thousand years ago Shaybānī, who lived and worked in what is now Iraq, wrote in his *Siyar* of the constraints on the use of force against other peoples; and centuries before even that, the *Bhagavad Gita* reflected the distinction drawn in Hinduism between righteous and unrighteous wars. Much effort was expended in crafting justifications for particular wars around such criteria. The speech given by Archbishop Chichele (after whom the Oxford chair in international law is named) in Act 1 of Shakespeare's *Henry V* in order to justify the war against France is but one example of the seriousness with which such exercises were taken—and an eerie foreshadowing of the tortured explanations of the justification for the war against Iraq in 2003.

The importance of there being a reasoned justification for the waging of a war appears to have been relatively constant throughout history—unsurprisingly, given that even individual homicides have, it seems, always been thought to demand some justification if they are not to be treated as serious crimes. What has changed, however, is the nature of the justification. Whereas the just war theorists focused upon substantive justifications for international wars, by the end of the 20th century the emphasis had moved from substance to procedure.

Fighting on the right occasions: the *jus ad bellum*

Until the 20th century there was no specific prohibition in international law on resort to war. The first general legal limitation on the use of force came in 1907, when the States participating in the Hague Peace Conference (initially convened by the Tsar of Russia in 1899) adopted the Hague Convention on the Limitation of Employment of Force for Recovery of Contract Debts. The States Parties to that Convention agreed 'not to have recourse to armed force for the recovery of contract debts claimed from the Government of one country by the Government of another country as being due to its citizens'. That commitment prohibited, for example, the sending of gunboats to blockade or bombard the coast of a debtor nation in order to impress upon its government the importance of paying its creditors. That practice was not uncommon during the 19th century; and as late as 1902–3, Britain, Germany, and Italy sent warships to blockade the coast of Venezuela, which had defaulted on debts owed to nationals of those States. (Venezuela subsequently agreed to commit a portion of its customs receipts to the repayment of its debts, and to submit certain disputes arising from the claims against it to arbitration, organized by the Permanent Court of Arbitration at The Hague.) The prohibition on the use of armed force in these circumstances was an echo of the old 'substantive' approach of just war doctrine to the question of limitations on war.

While the use of war as an instrument of debt collection was recognized to be unacceptable in 1907, it was not until after the First World War that the idea gained traction that the use of war as an instrument of foreign policy might be more generally outlawed. The move came with the creation in 1919, in large part as a result of the efforts of US President Woodrow Wilson, of the League of Nations. The League was created

> in order to promote international co-operation and to achieve international peace and security
>
> by the acceptance of obligations not to resort to war,
>
> by the prescription of open, just and honourable relations between nations,
>
> by the firm establishment of the understandings of international law as the actual rule of conduct among Governments, and
>
> by the maintenance of justice and a scrupulous respect for all treaty obligations in the dealings of organized peoples with one another.

That creed, set out in the preamble of the Covenant of the League, was the expression of a vision of the world order that had been spelled out in Wilson's 'Fourteen Points', itself a curious mixture of general principles (such as absolute freedom of navigation on the

6. Sometimes we expect too much. There are limits to what international organizations can achieve.

high seas) and specific recommendations (such as the creation of the League, and of a Polish State) presented in a speech to the US Congress at the beginning of 1918 as 'the programme of the world's peace' (see Figure 6).

The League Covenant adopted what now appears an almost naive approach to the imposition of legal limits upon the waging of war. In Article 12 of the Covenant, Members of the League agreed that they would submit disputes 'likely to lead to a rupture' either to arbitration or to the Council of the League for decision, and that they would not resort to war until three months after the arbitration award or Council report. League Members agreed not to go to war against Members complying with awards and unanimously adopted reports, and to impose trade and other sanctions immediately upon Members resorting to war in defiance of such awards or reports. The League Covenant thus sought to avert recourse to war, by imposing a cooling-off period and by offering protection to those who handled disputes within the League system; but it did not actually prohibit recourse to war. This is the shift from substance to procedure, which accompanied the creation of international organizations within which those procedures could be pursued.

The importance of that shift is immense. Current debates over the propriety of the use of force in contexts such as Iraq (2003) and Libya (2011), and the Middle East more generally (2014 and *passim*), frequently focus upon the question whether the necessary authorization has been secured from the United Nations or an appropriate regional organization, rather than upon the substantive moral justifications for the use of force. While that shift may provide a check against rash unilateral actions on the part of individual States, it allows important and difficult questions of morality—and, indeed, of military strategy and practicality—to be sidestepped. Attention focuses on what is permissible, at the expense of consideration of what is justifiable and helpful.

The limited constraint imposed by the League Covenant was taken a step further, outside the League apparatus, in the 1928 Treaty for the Renunciation of War (or the Kellogg–Briand Pact as it is sometimes called, after its main architects Frank B. Kellogg and Aristide Briand, the Foreign Ministers of the USA and of France). The 1928 Pact was adopted by Germany, the USA, France, Belgium, Great Britain and its Dominions, Italy, Japan, Poland, and the Czechoslovak Republic; and it was subsequently ratified by many more States, almost all of which were, within a dozen years, mired in the Second World War. Article 1 of the Pact provided that

The High Contracting Parties solemnly declare, in the names of their respective peoples, that they condemn recourse to war for the solution of international controversies and renounce it as an instrument of national policy in their relations with one another.

The scope of that self-imposed prohibition in the 1928 Pact was narrower than it might at first appear. The crucial qualification was spelled out by Sir Austen Chamberlain, the British Foreign Secretary (and, like Briand and Kellogg, a recipient of the Nobel Peace Prize), in a letter to the US Ambassador, in 1928:

The language of Article 1, as to the renunciation of war as an instrument of national policy, renders it desirable that I should remind your Excellency that there are certain regions of the world the welfare and integrity of which constitute a special and vital interest for our peace and safety. His Majesty's Government have been at pains to make it clear in the past that interference with these regions cannot be suffered. Their protection against attack is to the British Empire a measure of self-defence. It must be clearly understood that His Majesty's Government in Great Britain accept the new Treaty upon the distinct understanding that it does not prejudice their freedom of action in this respect.

Nonetheless, the Pact had taken a decisive step in departing—cases of self-defence apart—from the idea that resort to war could be justified by the (alleged) justness of the cause that the war was intended to advance.

The League scheme and the commitment to the renunciation of war were not great successes. Hampered from the start by the refusal of the US Senate to consent to the United States joining the League of Nations, both the League Covenant and the Kellogg–Briand Pact proved ineffective in the face of incidents such as the invasions of Manchuria and Abyssinia and the 1932 Chaco war between Bolivia and Paraguay, not to mention the

Second World War itself. But, despite the failures, it seemed that there could be no going back when the United Nations was established in 1945 to succeed the League. The deaths of many millions of people—not only the millions, mainly young men, who volunteered or were conscripted into national armies, but also the millions more men, women, and children who were the innocent victims of war—and the glimpses of destruction on a scale almost beyond comprehension in cities in Europe and Japan, made it inconceivable at that time that resort to war could be rehabilitated as a routine instrument of foreign policy.

When the Charter of the United Nations was drafted, with the hope of creating an effective international organization whose first purpose was 'to maintain international peace and security', the prohibition was extended beyond 'wars' to all uses of force, whether or not they were on a scale or of a nature to be regarded as a 'war' (and there was, in any event, no clear definition of what did count as a 'war' for legal purposes). Article 2(4) of the Charter thus stipulates that:

> All Members shall refrain in their international relations from the threat or use of force against the territorial integrity or political independence of any state, or in any other manner inconsistent with the Purposes of the United Nations.

But even here the prohibition is not absolute. Echoing the Chamberlain proviso of 1928, Article 51 of the Charter goes on to provide that:

> Nothing in the present Charter shall impair the inherent right of individual or collective self-defence if an armed attack occurs against a Member of the United Nations, until the Security Council has taken measures necessary to maintain international peace and security. Measures taken by Members in the exercise of this right of self-defence shall be immediately reported to the Security Council and shall not in any way affect the authority and responsibility of

the Security Council under the present Charter to take at any time such action as it deems necessary in order to maintain or restore international peace and security.

Article 51 preserves both the right of individual self-defence and the right of collective self-defence. The right of individual self-defence might be thought to be inherent. No legal system obliges people to sit passively and accept an unlawful attack upon themselves: there is always a right to take action in self-defence. (And legal principles common to all or most of the major legal systems of the world are regarded as a source of international law, in contexts where there may appear to be no other governing principle of treaty or customary international law.) The right of collective self-defence enables States to band together in defensive alliances, such as NATO (the North Atlantic Treaty Organization), established in 1949 to defend the West against threats from the Soviet Union and the East, and the Warsaw Pact, established in 1955 to defend the Soviet Union and the East against threats from NATO. The principles set out in Articles 2(4) and 51 of the Charter remain the framework within which international relations are conducted, insofar as the use of force is concerned.

Here again the approach to the regulation of armed force is essentially procedural. The Article 51 right of self-defence exists only 'until the Security Council has taken measures necessary to maintain international peace and security', and the focus thus shifts to the Security Council as the body which in any international crisis will quickly assume the responsibility for determining what, if any, force is to be used, and by whom.

The Security Council lies at the centre of the UN architecture. It consists of representatives of fifteen States: the five permanent members (the 'P5'), China, France, Russia, the UK, and the USA, and ten others elected for two-year terms by the UN General Assembly having regard to the contributions made by each State to the maintenance of international peace and security, and to the principle of the equitable geographical distribution of Security Council members.

It was intended by the drafters of the Charter, in the pre-Cold War years of the 1940s, that the Security Council should have at its disposal a standing UN military force which it could deploy as necessary in order to avert threats to international peace and security. That plan failed to materialize. Post-war austerity and Cold War pressures conspired to extinguish any possibility of such a permanent UN force, with the result that if the UN wishes to direct that military action be taken it must do so by calling upon Member States to place forces temporarily at its disposal. There have been more than sixty UN Peacekeeping Operations conducted on this basis since 1945, and UN forces remain in place in situations such as Cyprus, Lebanon, and Sudan. But the UN can only do what its Member States enable it to do; and the record of Member States in contributing to the UN is not very encouraging. As with all international organizations, we sometimes expect too much of it.

The Security Council has very extensive powers, particularly under Chapter VII of the Charter, which empowers the Council to impose legally binding obligations on Member States to implement measures, including the use of force, which it considers necessary for the purpose of maintaining or restoring international peace and security. The Council acts under Chapter VII when it imposes mandatory sanctions, such as trade embargoes or no-fly zones, upon miscreant States. But in the present context what is important is the fact that the deployment of force at the direction of the Security Council is a further exception, alongside the right of self-defence, to the basic prohibition on the use of force in international relations. This power was used, for example, to authorize US-led coalitions to take action against North Korea following its invasion of South Korea in 1950, and against Iraq following its invasion of Kuwait in 1990. It is, however, much more common for the UN to deploy forces which do not actually fight against one side in a conflict, but rather act as a buffer between the two warring sides, and which remain in place only so long as the State on whose territory they are stationed consents.

It was the legal protection allegedly offered by way of Security Council authorization that the United Kingdom and the United States sought to invoke prior to the invasion of Iraq in 2003, although the Security Council resolutions on which their argument depended appeared to most people to provide no warrant at all for that invasion. Nonetheless, the contorted arguments constructed by the UK and the USA were at least an indication that legality was a factor that they were taking into account. Better that than a view that the law did not matter and could be entirely ignored.

This does not exhaust the qualifications to the basic principle prohibiting the threat or use of force. On several occasions States have used limited force to rescue their nationals whose lives were in danger within the territory of another State. The Israeli operation in 1976 to rescue its nationals held hostage on a hijacked French aircraft that had landed at Entebbe airport in Uganda is one of the clearest examples. There was widespread, but by no means universal, support for the view that if the lives of a State's nationals are in grave and imminent danger abroad and the territorial State is unable or unwilling to act to secure their safety, the national State may itself use the minimum force necessary to rescue them. The inability and unwillingness of the territorial State is, however, difficult to establish (a problem which accounted for much of the disagreement over the Entebbe episode), and States always prefer to engage in such rescue missions with the consent of the territorial State if they can obtain it, rather than invoke the controversial right to act unilaterally.

A further limitation arises from the fact that the principle prohibiting the threat or use of force applies only in the context of international relations: governments may use force internally, within the State, without violating Article 2(4) of the UN Charter. This must be so, up to a point. If a group of protesters occupies government offices, no one would expect international law to forbid their eviction, even if it involved the use of force—subject, of course, to limits upon the kind and degree of force that is used, which is ultimately constrained by rules of human rights law. If the protesters dig in and arm themselves, the force necessary to eject them may be considerable. It may be that the government cannot regain control and restore its authority without outside assistance, whether that be from some Mephistophelian arms dealer or from a supportive State. It is perfectly lawful to give such assistance to incumbent governments. Indeed, if the assistance maintains the authority of a legitimate government and so promotes international stability, it is likely to receive widespread approbation. There is, however, a limit to this logic.

While international law does not say that there comes a point where a government must actually give up and yield control of all or part of its territory to insurgents, it does say that when the conflict reaches the level of a civil war, outside States must not intervene and must not assist either the government or the insurgents (for example, by supplying either side with armaments). This stance is rooted in the conception of internal sovereignty. The principle is that the people of each State have the right to determine their own future, and not to have that future determined or imposed by the military intervention of third States. The right is, of course, imperfect: third States are free to choose what political and economic links they would have with a restored government or with a new government established by the insurgents, and that choice may have a decisive influence upon the viability of the successful party in a civil war. Nonetheless, international law does at least seek to exclude the most egregious examples of the installation of puppet regimes and proxy wars.

The law does not stand still. Customary law, in particular, is constantly adjusting to changing situations and expectations. The move towards the establishment of a right of humanitarian intervention is a case in point. In the face of harrowing reports of ethnic cleansing and massive human rights violations in the former Yugoslavia in the late 1990s, neighbouring States appeared to have no legal basis upon which they could intervene. The conflict did not directly threaten them, so no right to use force in self-defence was available. The incumbent government, in Serbia, was certainly not inviting the use of force against it. The Security Council had not authorized the use of force. Those in danger were not identified as nationals of the outside States. And yet in the aerial bombing campaign that began in March 1999, NATO launched over 10,000 air strikes against Serbian forces in the Serbian province of Kosovo. Differing views were taken of the legality of this action, not least because it was an unexpected extension of the prescribed scope of the NATO powers as a collective self-defence organization. Perhaps the most accurate characterization of the campaign is that it was an action which the participating States considered to be morally and politically justified, and that those imperatives overrode whatever doubts there might have been concerning its legality under the established rules of international law. Some would go further and argue that the campaign was an exercise of a legal right of humanitarian intervention, though it is very doubtful if any such right antedated the Kosovo bombings.

The episode is a classic case of the development of international law in response to situations for which existing rules are ill suited. The idea that neighbouring States should be obliged by law to stand by and watch the most appalling and systematic large-scale human rights abuses is one that would lead many people to say that the law must be changed (and also to ask what is the point of maintaining huge standing armies if they do nothing to avert such atrocities). The UN Charter could, in theory, be renegotiated to

74

create a further exception to Article 2(4), permitting the use of force if it is necessary to prevent massive and serious human rights violations; but renegotiation would take a long time, and it is probable that there would be enormous difficulty in obtaining agreement on the definition of a provision that would permit militarily powerful States to intervene in weaker States. By taking unilateral action and offering a reasoned justification for it, however, the proponents of such intervention can try to launch a new rule of customary international law.

If other States accept or acquiesce in the action, it will become accepted as action that is consistent with international law; and as evidence of support for the rule gathers and hardens, a new right will emerge. If, on the other hand, the action meets overwhelmingly with protests and objections, it will not pass into customary international law. It is true that in principle, even if there is a right in customary international law to engage in such novel action, it would not free States of their obligations under more restrictive treaties, including Article 2(4) of the UN Charter. But international law is nothing if not pragmatic. It is recognized that the Charter is an organic, evolving structure; and modifications of this kind are tolerated and absorbed into international practice. The 'humanitarian intervention' in Kosovo, which was not condemned (but was not expressly condoned) by the Security Council, appears to be gaining wider acceptance, as calls for intervention in other situations, such as the Great Lakes conflict in Africa and the situations in the Middle East, demonstrate.

I have focused on the right of States to be free of armed intervention from outside, and on clear cases involving that right. As is the case with all legal rules, however, there is a penumbra, an area where it is not entirely clear whether actions do or do not fall under the prohibition. For example, what of economic coercion, such as suspending trade links or government loans, but not involving armed force? Here the answer is tolerably clear.

Attempts to bring economic coercion explicitly within legal definitions of aggression and unlawful armed force have been made and have failed; and while economic coercion may in some cases violate international trade rules (including WTO rules) and the principle of non-intervention (to which I shall shortly turn), as a matter of law it is not equated to uses of armed force.

To take another example, does assistance for rebels within a State violate the prohibition on the threat or use of force in Article 2(4)? What if the assistance consists in training the rebels, or arming them, or only in financing them? These questions were discussed by the International Court in the *Nicaragua* case in 1986, in a judgment upholding Nicaragua's complaint that the USA had acted unlawfully in supporting the Contra rebels in their fight against the Sandinista government. The higher levels of involvement may amount to indirect uses of force in violation of Article 2(4); and a much wider range of assistance than that will violate the principle of non-intervention.

Before turning to the question of non-intervention, I should say something about the degree of compliance with the international law on the use of force. The catalogue of exceptions may leave the prohibition on the use of force looking a little ragged: self-defence; Security Council authorization; rescues of nationals (perhaps); force used by incumbent governments; humanitarian intervention (perhaps). In practice, however, the prohibition on the use of force in international relations is remarkably well established.

It may seem disingenuous to write of a general international practice of following the prohibition on the threat or use of force, given episodes such as the conflicts in Vietnam, the Middle East, the Great Lakes region of Africa, Sri Lanka, Iraq, Afghanistan, Georgia, Ukraine—the list goes on and on. But what is crucial for the emergence and survival of the legal principle is not its complete observance but rather the fact that what may appear to be (and may in fact be) violations of the rules should be explained by the States involved in terms that implicitly affirm, rather than deny, the continuing validity of the rule.

Thus, when Israel and its Arab neighbours fought in the Six-Day War in 1967, both sides claimed to be acting in self-defence and therefore in accordance with Article 51 of the Charter, and not in violation of the prohibition on the use of force set out in Article 2(4). Similarly, when the USSR (as it then was) invaded Afghanistan in 1980, and the USA invaded Grenada in 1983, it was claimed that the intervening State had been invited in by the legitimate government of the State concerned. If those claims were true, the interventions would have been consistent with international law because, as I explained above, self-defence and the provision of military assistance at the request of an incumbent government are outside the international law prohibition on the use of force. From the point of view of the stability of the Rule of Law what matters more than the question whether the claims were in fact true is the fact that the episode is explained in a way that purports to demonstrate that the intervening State acted within the rules of international law. In that way the importance of the rules, and the continued respect for the rules, is signalled. Hypocrisy is the tribute that weak and sinful man pays to the law. The time to become really worried is when States do not care whether their actions are lawful or not.

There is another point, even more fundamental, to recall. It is that the appraisal of action by reference to the standards of the law is something that we choose to do: it is not inevitable. This is so obvious at the domestic level as often to be overlooked. If a dispute arises with a neighbour, only a sociopath would turn immediately to the law to resolve it. The natural response is to discuss it and to reach a practical accommodation which may bear no relation to the respective legal rights and duties of the parties. Even police forces and regulatory agencies routinely go about the business of 'enforcing' the law by informal means. The fact is that the cost to society, and to all the individuals involved, of pursuing legal remedies for every wrong would be practically all-consuming. No society could function on that basis. One chooses which disputes are best handled through formal legal procedures and which disputes are not.

It is much the same with international law. Some disputes are treated as legal, and a solution in line with international law is demanded. This was the case with the Iraqi invasion of Kuwait. Other disputes are treated as essentially 'political', so that the search for a settlement is by no means limited to the range of solutions that give effect to the rights and duties of the Parties. The situation of the Palestinians is an example. For decades, negotiations have been couched not in terms of what international law requires or forbids but rather in terms of what concessions might reasonably be expected or made. It is an interesting question whether there is a coherent set of principles—meta-principles—hovering above law and *realpolitik* alike, and directing disputes down one or other track, legal or extra-legal; or whether the lesson is that in every legal system there comes a point where a determination to disobey the law is unassailable because there is no realistic possibility of the community being able to marshal the resources that would be necessary for an attempt to coerce the parties into compliance with the law. Put another way, law is ultimately no more than one among several frameworks from which we may choose, within which conflicts may be adjusted.

Non-intervention

In much the same way that the most widespread and pernicious forms of domestic abuse are (arguably) not physical violence but the application of psychological and financial pressure, the use of force is not the biggest threat to the principles of autonomy and equal dignity in international relations.

I noted in the previous section that although economic aggression was not regarded as falling within the scope of uses of the force proscribed by international law, it could amount to a violation of the prohibition on intervention in the internal affairs of other States. Article 2(7) of the UN Charter stipulates that nothing in the Charter 'shall authorize the United Nations to intervene in matters which are essentially within the domestic jurisdiction of any State', except insofar as this results from measures taken by the Security Council under Chapter VII of the Charter. The clear implication is that the UN should not interfere in a State's internal affairs; and there is a general understanding that, similarly, no State should interfere in another's internal affairs. Again like domestic abuse, what goes on behind the front door is, on this view, no one else's business.

While the non-intervention principle may remain more or less intact, the notion of what amounts to 'internal affairs' and the point at which something becomes a matter of broader public concern have undergone profound changes. The most obvious development has been the growth of international (as opposed to national) human rights law. During the first half of the 20th century there were many cases before international tribunals in which States were held liable for failures to observe the international minimum standard of treatment of foreign nationals, for example by failing to provide basic protection against mob violence or to investigate crimes committed against foreigners. But the way that a State treated its own nationals was not regarded as a matter of international law or as a proper concern of other States.

The shock and outrage at the revelation of industrial-scale killings, not only in Nazi Germany but under other savage and ruthless regimes too, changed this perception. Genuine concern to secure basic human rights, coupled with a desire to tie down governments whose treacherous abuse of their own citizens could easily trigger international conflict, created an atmosphere that was unusually receptive to idealistic projects. During the 1940s and 1950s, seminal texts such as the Universal Declaration on Human Rights (1948) and the European Convention on Human Rights (1950) were not only drafted but solemnly adopted by States. The European Convention created a mechanism by which one State Party could take another before the European Court of Human Rights alleging that it was failing to observe its human rights commitments even in its own territory. The cases brought by Ireland against the UK, by Cyprus against Turkey, and by Georgia against Russia, are among the cases brought on this basis. Less prominently, but much more commonly, States make public criticisms or diplomatic representations to each other concerning human rights issues. Though these are sometimes rebuffed as unwelcome, few would now say that such statements are actually unlawful interferences in internal affairs, incompatible with States' duties under international law.

As the interdependence of States becomes ever more apparent, the category of domestic actions which are regarded as matters in which foreign States have a legitimate interest is steadily growing. Environmental and economic problems can rarely be confined within national borders, and while the core principle of the independence and autonomy of each State remains intact, its application is tempered by the increasing appreciation that even in the exercise of their independence, through choices concerning the use of resources and economic policies, States cannot behave without regard for the consequences for their neighbours.

Sanctions

Sometimes States do not stop at words, but try overtly to force another State to change the way in which it behaves. Pressure may be applied by withholding foreign aid, imposing restrictions on imports or exports, imposing travel bans on named individuals, and similar acts of retorsion.

Sometimes the pressure may take the form of action that is a prima facie violation of international law, such as an asset freeze in which dealings with property located within the jurisdiction of the State taking the counter-measures—for example deposits in bank accounts belonging to the wrongdoing State or to particular individuals or companies associated with it—are forbidden. Such interferences are tantamount to seizures of foreign property, and are lawful only because they are justified as counter-measures, or are imposed as sanctions mandated by the UN Security Council.

If ordered by the UN Security Council the duty to implement such sanctions can be made binding upon all States because that is the rule set out in Chapter VII of the UN Charter, which all States accept when they become Members of the United Nations. In practice, it is more common for sanctions to be orchestrated by individual States and their allies, or by regional organizations such as the European Union and ECOWAS (the Economic Community of West African States). To the extent that such non-UN sanctions would in principle violate international law, they are justified as counter-measures.

Sanctions are often criticized as a blunt instrument that hurts the poor and weak more than those individuals who are actually responsible for the wrongdoing of miscreant States. In recent decades much effort has been put in to the fashioning of 'smart' or 'targeted' sanctions, aimed at strategic industries and transactions, and at key institutions and members of the ruling elite within the State. Such targeted sanctions can be very specific, as in the case of the ban on exports of Rolex watches to North Korea imposed in 2006, which was aimed practically personally at Kim Jong-il, then Head of State. But the 'smartness' of sanctions is far from perfect. Apart from the fact that ingenious and lucrative schemes for evading sanctions almost inevitably spring up, problems arising from the inconsistent transliteration of names from non-Latin scripts and from the common refusal of States on security grounds to explain why individuals are included in lists of sanctions targets can give even targeted sanctions regimes a quality more reminiscent of Kafka's judges than of the precision engineer.

Economic sanctions may lack the immediacy of the expeditions of gunboats, such as the European warships that blockaded Venezuela in 1902 when it refused to repay its foreign debt. But, while uses of military force to try to compel States to change their behaviour are widely regarded as an anachronistic and unpalatable form of bullying, trade sanctions can inflict much greater damage on the target State. Moreover, the prohibition of supplies of goods and services to a State is often a very indiscriminate tool. Even if food, clothes, and medicines are exempted from the bans, shortages of fuel and machine parts can quickly reduce levels of economic activity. Lack of employment, money, and transportation, and deteriorating infrastructure, can rapidly lead to sickness and poverty and cause severe hardship.

To take one example, while estimates vary widely most accept that the number of deaths resulting from economic sanctions against Iraq during the confrontation with Saddam Hussein must be measured at least in the tens of thousands. The Office of the UN High Commissioner for Human Rights reported in 2000 that the maternal mortality rate in Iraq increased from 50/100,000 live births in 1989 to 117/100,000 in 1997, while the infant mortality rate rose from 64/1,000 births in 1990 to 129/1,000 in 1995. The governing elites responsible for the errant behaviour of States are usually able to ensure that they themselves suffer relatively little from these effects. The weak and the poor, in contrast, are particularly vulnerable, and may bear the greatest weight of the hardships that the sanctions are intended to inflict. Economic sanctions may appear more 'peaceful' than military force; but they inflict their own form of suffering.

The limitations on the right to use such force are a key element among the principles by which international law secures the sovereign equality and independence of States against external threats. Chapter 5 pursues that theme, examining the principles of international law that spell out in positive terms the content of that equality and independence.

Chapter 5
Sovereignty inside the State

Why States still matter

Politicians are fond of referring to 'our way of life' and to the 'values' that underpin the State. Many people would question the idea that there is much in the way of a coherent body of values that are established and pursued across divisions of class, age, gender, religion, language, and ethnicity within a single State—to take only the most obvious social divisions that exist in States all around the world. Nonetheless, we do usually think of the rest of the world in terms of 'foreign' States and 'foreign' nationalities, and of the facile stereotypes that make nationality such a potent concept.

Increasingly, one might question whether nationality is the grouping that really matters. Governmental powers, economies, cultures, and many other social phenomena exist at local, provincial, national, regional, and continental levels; and it is at least arguable that the devolution of powers from the national to the local level, and the drift of powers from national governments to supranational bodies such as the organs of the European Union, is steadily eroding the practical significance of the nation-State from above and below. Indeed, it is not fanciful to view the EU, NATO, attempts to establish an Islamic caliphate in the Middle East, and attempts to persuade States to stand together to defend 'western values' as all being manifestations (among many others) of the same perception: that the nation-State is not the size or kind of social unit that is best suited to each and every one of the agendas and aspirations of its citizens and of those who govern them.

The answer to questions about the continuing utility of nationality obviously depends upon how one tests 'what matters'. It is probably true that, as a matter of fact, most inhabitants of the planet, most of the time, are not concerned with questions of international affairs or international economic or social policies. Life is generally lived locally, within a local rather than a national or international framework. Nonetheless, when action is required, to alleviate the effects of poverty or disease or flooding or drought, for example, one still looks primarily to national governments. They are the bodies that raise and spend most taxes, and that have most control over armed forces and over the roads and railways, the schools and hospitals, and so on upon which the citizens depend. National governments have the most control over matters such as immigration and emigration and international trade. Even in relation to matters such as policing and power supplies, in which local or regional authorities may be the primary controllers and determiners of policies and priorities, national governments usually have a degree of overarching or residual control that makes them the natural focus of social power and activity.

It is arguably the control of legislatures and taxation that makes national governments pre-eminent among the social institutions whose actions mould the character of everyday life. By stipulating in laws what must and what must not be done, and by exercising its control over the resources necessary to do those things, the national government—and with it, the nation-State—retains its primary importance. When one adds the special position of the national government's ministry of foreign affairs, which is the accepted contact point with foreign governments, the case for a focus upon the nation-State becomes overwhelming, no matter how active and flourishing informal trade and social links with foreign groups might be.

This is where the legal concepts of territorial sovereignty and of jurisdiction play a crucial role. Each State has the sovereign right to decide upon its social and economic structures, and to lay down laws that will have a major influence on the national character of the State and of life within it. The legal concept of jurisdiction determines the reach and priority of those laws. It sets the limits within which a State has the right to prescribe such rules, and also within which a State has the right to enforce them.

Jurisdiction and the State

The basic principle is that jurisdiction is territorial: that is, the legislature of a State has the primary right to set the laws that apply to everyone within the borders of the territory of that State. It is an aspect of territorial sovereignty, and of the right of self-determination set out in instruments such as the 1966 International Covenants on Civil and Political Rights and on Economic, Social and Cultural Rights, that States and peoples have the right to pursue their own economic, social, and cultural development, freely choosing the legal structures that support them.

It is this freedom that entitles the government of a State to decide if the *burqa* may be worn in public places, to choose to prohibit the sale or consumption of alcohol or opium, or the production of graven images or seditious or pornographic material, and to stipulate how many spouses each person may have and how old they must be, and whether citizens must pay for their own education or healthcare or transportation, and so on. The primacy of territorial jurisdiction and the freedom to choose the social structure secures the right of societies to be different.

That freedom is not unlimited: it is constrained by obligations of the State under international law, of which the most significant in practice are those arising from human rights laws and from various trade and economic agreements that provide rights for people to enter and work in the States Parties to them.

The European Convention on Human Rights ('ECHR') is, alongside the similar Inter-American and African conventions, one of the major regional human rights conventions. The States Parties to those conventions have chosen to bind themselves to secure certain fundamental human rights for all people within their jurisdiction—which, in the case of the ECHR, includes not only the territory of a State but also areas and situations abroad that are under the control of the State, as the so-called 'Turkish Republic of Northern Cyprus' is under Turkish control and jurisdiction, and British military personnel and the prisons that they operated in Iraq during the second Iraq War were under British control and jurisdiction. The right to life, the prohibitions on torture and arbitrary detention and punishment, the rights to freedom of thought and expression, and the prohibitions on discrimination are among the rights and duties secured by the ECHR and other human rights instruments; and the list has been greatly augmented by the adoption of protocols adding to the basic convention rights and, above all, by the exegetical decisions of the European Court of Human Rights and its equivalents elsewhere.

Like all treaty obligations, States' obligations under the ECHR are self-imposed. They bind only those States that have chosen to become Parties to the ECHR; and it is wrong to suggest that they are somehow foisted upon Member States—though it must be admitted that it is unlikely that all States foresaw the extent to which the ECtHR would apply the broad principles of the ECHR's fundamental rights to the minutiae of everyday life. Moreover, even if the ECtHR (which is a Council of Europe body, quite separate from the European Union) declares that a particular decision or law of a Member State is incompatible with the ECHR, that ruling does not automatically override national law. A State in breach of the ECHR is obliged as a matter of international law to take steps to bring itself into conformity with its ECHR obligations: but if the State does not do so, the State's own courts and authorities will comply with national law. Only if the State's own national law directs its courts and authorities to give precedence to the ECHR (or any other international obligation) over inconsistent national laws will they give the ECHR such precedence. And if the ECHR is thought to be too intrusive in its intervention into national legal systems, the Member States have it in their power to amend it—though it is well to remember that the ECHR rights were defined by those who fought in and survived the Second World War as a bulwark against the slide into State terror: it is not lightly to be put aside. But for as long as States choose to remain Parties to the ECHR, it will undeniably constrain the States' freedom to legislate as they choose.

This is not only true of human rights obligations: all treaty obligations constrain the States Parties to some extent. To take another example, Bilateral Investment Treaties ('BITs'), of which there are between two and three thousand worldwide, are very significant restrictions on what the States Parties can do in relation to investors from the other State. BITs typically prohibit discrimination against the foreign investors and require that they be accorded 'fair and equitable treatment'. The latter requirement is particularly trenchant: even if an investor is treated in a non-discriminatory manner in accordance with the host State's laws, it will be entitled to a remedy if it suffers loss as a result of some action which, though lawful, is unfair. An example would be the abandonment by a State of a commitment to maintain a particular tax regime, made to an investor who relied upon it in deciding to make the investment.

Accession to bodies such as the World Trade Organization ('WTO') and the International Monetary Fund ('IMF') have similar consequences. States may find themselves bound under international law not to provide subsidies to domestic industries, even indirectly through mechanisms such as tax breaks or subsidized energy supplies, and not to impose currency controls; and such constraints may have a considerable impact upon the government's freedom to choose its own economic policies. The point is well illustrated by the mass of international disputes that arose from the Latin American debt crises around the turn of the millennium, when investors and creditors invoked their rights against the governments of the States concerned. Scores of cases were brought against Latin American States by foreign investors before arbitration tribunals, as they were entitled to do under the terms of applicable BITs.

The sovereignty of a State is accordingly a central concept. Externally, with the aspect facing out to the rest of the world, it establishes the right of the State in principle to legislate as it chooses, and to build its own chosen kind of social, economic, and political order. But it also gives the legal capacity to enter into the very binding agreements which constrain the State's freedom of action. And internally, with the aspect of sovereignty that faces inwards to a State's citizens and courts and authorities, it gives the State the legal power to do what it chooses, consistently with the constitutional law of the State, even if that involves acting contrary to the State's international obligations.

Jurisdiction and territory

Every State has jurisdiction over its territory. That is obvious, and practically tautological given the concept of Statehood with which international law operates. The territory of the State is the whole of the area within its borders, and also the adjacent territorial sea, up to 12 miles from the coast. It includes the airspace above and the subsoil below. A State's airspace, in this context, is usually reckoned to extend up to the edge of the atmosphere, around 100 kilometres above the earth, beyond which is Outer Space, an area where international law (as understood by earthlings, at least) does not recognize that any State may gain exclusive rights. By a long-established legal fiction, ships and aircraft are also treated for jurisdictional purposes as if they are part of the territory of the State in which they are registered—the flag State—which may extend its laws to them as it chooses.

Jurisdiction at sea is a little more complicated. The territorial sea of a State (together with its seabed and the airspace above it) is regarded as being as much a part of its territory as is its land, though foreign ships have a limited right of navigation (innocent passage) through it; but beyond the 12-mile limit at sea matters are rather different. Until the late 20th century all the waters beyond the territorial sea were treated as high seas, free for use by ships of any State for fishing, navigation, overflight or any other lawful purpose. (Some States claimed 3-mile territorial seas with jurisdiction in a contiguous zone in respect of customs and fishing for a few miles beyond that; others claimed a 6- or 12-mile territorial sea; but there were no serious claims to a coastal belt wider than 12 miles.) There was thus a stark contrast between the territorial sea, in which a coastal State could exercise jurisdiction over all ships, regardless of their nationality, and the high seas, where (with the exception of ships engaged in piracy) ships were subject to the jurisdiction of their flag State alone.

In the 1940s States, recognizing the strategic importance of offshore oil supplies, began to claim exclusive rights over the continental shelf—the relatively shallow seabed beyond the limits of the territorial sea that is the seaward extension of the land mass of continents and islands, as distinct from the deep ocean floor. The USA, which led that move, has an extensive continental shelf; and the shallow waters of the Gulf of Mexico were an early target of the petroleum industry. The US lead was followed by other States, each unilaterally asserting its ownership of the resources of the continental shelf, and because of the generality of that practice and the absence of any significant opposition to it a new rule of customary international law swiftly emerged. States in areas such as the west coast of South America, however, have very narrow shelves and stood to gain little from the appropriation of the seabed resources. A parallel trend began in which those States asserted rights not only over the seabed resources, but also over the whole of the water column out to 200 miles measured from their coasts. Those claims were opposed by the traditional naval States, including the victorious allied powers in the Second World War (which were also major colonial powers), in particular because the claims were seen to threaten the high seas freedoms such as navigation and fishing from which they benefited greatly, and the opposition precluded the general acceptance of the practice that was necessary to generate new customary international law.

During the 1970s, however, the re-emergence into independent Statehood of many former colonies, coupled with the growing realization that the free-for-all high seas regime was leading to the serious over-fishing of commercial fish stocks, and that other interests in the seas (such as rights of navigation and overflight) could in fact be reconciled with the coastal State ownership of marine resources that was in practice necessary if rational resource management regimes were to be put in place, led to a radical change in the law. Following clear signs of a generally accepted change in State practice, the 1982 UN Convention on the Law of the Sea, which provides a comprehensive legal framework for the use of the seas, reflected this change by providing that each coastal State is entitled to exercise jurisdiction over the living resources (fish, whales, etc.) and non-living resources (oil, gas, gravel, placer deposits, etc.) of the sea and seabed, and over certain other matters including pollution, scientific research, and artificial islands and other installations (such as oil rigs, offshore waste disposal plants, and wind turbines), in a 200-mile exclusive economic zone ('EEZ') adjacent to its coasts. As part of the package deal that rendered this move acceptable to the traditional naval States, freedom of navigation and overflight was expressly preserved, in particular through key strategic straits such as the Straits of Gibraltar.

These developments regarding marine resources have a spatial aspect: they gave to coastal States new and extended maritime zones. But in essence they were jurisdictional, rather than territorial, developments. The EEZ is not actually a part of the territory of a State: it is an (admittedly, geographically defined) area within which the coastal State has a limited jurisdictional competence, tied to the resources (hence the name 'economic' zone) of the zone, including what may at first sight not seem like resources at all—economic goods such as wind power, and the cleanliness of the seas. The jurisdiction of the coastal State in its EEZ does, however, give it the ability to control and legislate for the exploration and exploitation of those resources.

The jurisdiction of a State means that it may regulate the conduct of all persons, regardless of their nationality, within its territory. The idea of conduct 'within the territory' of a State is more elusive than might be supposed. Sometimes States seek to extend their legislative jurisdiction over activities abroad that produce consequences within their territory. There is no significant problem with the archetypal examples of crimes that are partly located outside the territory of a State, such as cross-frontier shootings or postal crimes. If a person in Switzerland shoots someone across the border in France, or posts a blackmailing letter to that person, both Switzerland (as the State where the crime is initiated) and France (as the place where the crime is completed) would be entitled to exercise jurisdiction: they have concurrent jurisdiction over the whole crime, elements of which were committed in the territory of each of them. But the position with non-physical consequences is much less easy. What if the consequences are intangible and abstract?

The United States was particularly active in asserting jurisdiction on the basis of non-physical consequences affecting US territory or interests. For example, it penalized under its antitrust laws the organization of cartels outside the USA by non-US businesses, if the cartel had an effect upon competition in US markets. Such extensions of jurisdiction have often proved controversial. What may appear in New York to be an attempt by, say, a group of European companies to cartelize the US market may appear in Europe to be rational cooperation in order to compete successfully in US markets. Which view should prevail?

One might try to divide the situation up along territorial lines, and say that companies can cooperate in Europe, but that the USA retains the right to penalize any adverse effects of that cooperation that are proved actually to have been sustained on US territory without, however, ordering the cooperation to cease. But the problem is that in many situations the location of the 'effects' cannot be pinpointed, and that it is not possible to isolate the parts of an offence that occur within a State's territory and allow it to regulate them but not conduct outside the territory. For example, the effect of a cartel upon competition in foreign markets is a diffuse economic force. Even if the members of the cartel, in fixing standard conditions of supply or in carving up sales territories between them, had, say, the USA primarily in mind, the economic results of the cooperation between them might well have affected the markets in, say, Canada and Mexico and Russia, too. Can each of them penalize the cartel? And what if (as is not uncommon) some of the States, including their home States in Europe, actually encourage commercial cooperation in respect of foreign markets, in order to boost exports? Can the USA prohibit European companies from doing things in Europe that are actually encouraged by the EU itself?

Such problems are far from uncommon. Similar difficulties arise from the fact that so many transactions now involve electronic transmissions routed through servers in different countries. Many large international banking transactions pass through the computers of the US-based Clearing House Interbank Payments

System ('CHIPS'). Is the shuffling of electrons in a computer in New York (or wherever the servers in the network of computers may be located) sufficient to found US territorial jurisdiction over the transaction that it helps to execute? If the USA imposes sanctions on a State or individual who is the intended recipient of a transfer from an account in a British bank, and that transfer would routinely pass through the CHIPS system, would it be caught by US sanctions legislation? What if the UK had adopted no such sanctions, and neither the transferor nor the transferee had any contact with the United States and had no reason to suppose that US law might impede the making of the payment?

Those problems arise from the fact that a particular activity may involve elements occurring in several different States. Differences in the attitudes of those States to the activity can cause jurisdictional conflicts. Such conflicts can also arise because States assert jurisdiction not only on the basis of territoriality, but on the basis of other links between the State and the regulated conduct. The longest and most firmly established such link is between the State and the persons who have its nationality.

Jurisdiction and persons

These days we naturally think of the duty to conform in territorial terms: 'when in Rome, do as the Romans do.' In most early societies, however, social organization was based on the tribe or family rather than on particular geographical locations. The duty of obedience to 'the law' was personal: each individual was bound loyally to obey the commands of his overlord and king, wherever the king and his courtiers might wander. That deeply rooted human convention survives in the international legal system.

As a matter of international law, each State is entitled to make laws that its citizens must obey whether they are at home or abroad; and some crimes have a gravity that is considered by lawmakers to demand the prosecution of their perpetrators wherever they may have been committed. For instance, some States make it a criminal offence for their nationals to travel abroad in order to engage in the sexual exploitation of children, whether or not a particular activity is a crime in the foreign State where it is actually carried out. Treason, bigamy, and murder also fell into this category. More recently, narcotics trafficking, money laundering, piracy, and terrorism laws have also commonly been given what is known as 'extraterritorial' effect—that is, they apply to nationals of the State even when they are outside the territory of the State—reflecting the practical need to approach at least some forms of criminal activity on the basis that they are frequently international by nature, and do not have the localized focus of crimes such as theft and assault. A few States have also asserted jurisdiction over crimes committed abroad whenever the victims (rather than the perpetrators) have the nationality of the State; but such assertions have tended to attract widespread support only in respect of certain terrorist offences, such as hostage-taking.

It is often said that some crimes are regarded as so serious that, as a matter of international law, any State may prosecute a suspected perpetrator, wherever the offence was allegedly committed and even if the alleged perpetrator is not a national of that State. This 'universal' jurisdiction attached to piracy and slavery, both of them offences now enjoying something of a renaissance, and various 'crimes against humanity' such as genocide, grave breaches of the laws of war, and torture. In truth, it is hard to see that the 'seriousness' of these crimes explains universal jurisdiction over them. For example, piracy is not necessarily any more serious than any other form of armed robbery; and it is hard to explain why only the acts overseen by public officials count as torture, and not similar acts carried out by the enforcers of drug cartels and other criminal groups (although it is likely that quasi-governmental gangs imposing their own species of 'order' upon territories where there is no effective regular government will be assimilated to public officials in this context).

The main reason that certain crimes came to be subject to universal jurisdiction under customary international law is opportunistic. There are many crimes that are appalling and universally condemned; but in a much smaller category of cases it is common for the alleged perpetrators to have a considerable freedom to travel, whether because they operate (like pirates and the slave traders of old) at sea or because they have enjoyed the fruits of power and corruption within—and the practical ability to leave—the States where they have committed their crimes. In such cases the perpetrators often escape prosecution at home. These have been the kinds of people singled out for assertions of universal jurisdiction in the past. Indeed, they still are. There have been quite a number of attempts to arrest alleged 'war criminals', for example, when they have been on trips to London or New York or Paris or some other city where swift justice is open to all, including vigilant groups of political and human rights activists.

These days, it is much more common for extraterritorial jurisdiction over persons to arise by treaty than under customary international law. States will try to fabricate an international consensus and to adopt an international convention on the repression of certain defined crimes. The States Parties to such treaties, which apply to offences such as torture, corruption, and genocide, typically agree that any of them may prosecute offences committed in another State, unless they extradite the accused person to face prosecution abroad—usually in the State where the alleged offence was committed. The principle known as *aut dedere, aut judicare*—either hand over the person to another State that wants him or put his case to the prosecuting authorities of the State where he is found—has done much to encourage States to initiate inquiries into crimes that in the past may well have escaped investigation.

Jurisdiction and property

There have been occasional attempts to extend jurisdiction over other 'things' which are in essence treated as if they are property rights. Rights under the law of the sea over the EEZ resources might be looked upon as one example. Another is the rule of international law that has long permitted States to criminalize the counterfeiting of their currency by aliens abroad, as if there were some kind of intellectual property right that each State is entitled to protect in its currency. But when the USA attempted to extend its jurisdiction over goods incorporating significant proportions of US technology, prohibiting anyone, anywhere from selling such goods without US government permission to certain proscribed destinations as part of its sanctions programme, other States objected. To order a research establishment in Oxford not to sell to London University a super-computer bought from a US supplier without US permission, and to make that permission conditional upon students of certain nationalities not being allowed access to the computer, was a step too far. Plugging leaks in sanctions regimes is a classic role for international cooperation, not something that can be achieved unilaterally without treading on the toes—without invading the sovereign independence—of other States. The jurisdiction of States remains overwhelmingly territorial in its focus, although the duties of citizenship may tie individuals to their national laws as they travel around the world.

Enforcing the law

It is one thing to prescribe laws, another to enforce them. Enforcement jurisdiction is strictly territorial. While a State may make it an offence for one of its nationals to participate abroad in the planning of terrorist attacks, for example, the State cannot send its police into the foreign country to arrest that national. If it did send them in, without the permission of the foreign State, it would violate the sovereignty of the foreign State. Indeed, that sometimes happens: there are infamous examples of US drug enforcement officers crossing the border to seize wanted persons in Mexico, and taking them back surreptitiously to the USA, on occasion drugged and concealed in crates. Usually, however, States observe the proprieties of international law and if a State wants to prosecute someone for an offence committed abroad (or even for an offence committed within its own territory, if the suspected offender has fled abroad), it will request the return of that person. If the suspect does not return voluntarily, he may be arrested by the authorities in the State in which he is living and extradited to the State that wishes to prosecute him.

Most States will only extradite wanted persons if there is an extradition treaty in force between the requesting and the requested State. Such treaties, which may be bilateral or multilateral, or regional arrangements such as the European Arrest Warrant, typically only provide for extradition in relation to relatively serious offences, punishable by imprisonment for a certain minimum period. Some States refuse to extradite their own nationals under any circumstances; and most States refuse to extradite people who can show that they are being prosecuted for 'political' reasons such as opposition to the requesting regime.

Though the rules are quite distinct, the non-extradition of political offenders complements the principles of international law relating to refugees—that is, people who fear persecution in their national State because of their 'race, religion, nationality, membership of a particular social group or political opinion'. The Convention on the Status of Refugees, adopted in 1951 in the wake of the horrors of the Second World War and broadened in scope by a Protocol adopted in 1967, does not actually give refugees the right to enter another State in order to seek asylum. It says only that if they are in another State and do seek asylum, the authorities there may not return the asylum seeker to the frontiers of territories where his life or freedom would be threatened on account of any of the listed characteristics. The paradox of making what is widely, if inaccurately, thought of as the 'right to asylum' dependent upon what will often be an irregular entry into, or stay in, the State where asylum is sought is one (but not the only) factor that underlies the appalling trade in human misery and desperation which passes under the name of 'migrant smuggling'.

When laws collide

What happens when laws collide—when, say, State A legislates on the basis of territoriality and State B on the basis of nationality, and a person is caught between conflicting demands (see Figure 7)? Who has the power to decide if women must, or must not, wear a full-face veil—the *burqa*—in France, or may choose whether or not to do so? What if the French legislature enacts a law that forbids the wearing of the *burqa*, but some other State or other body (such as a religious authority) says that wearing a *burqa* is mandatory, and perhaps imposes penalties on those women who do not wear them? May any individual be punished by the respective authorities both for wearing and for not wearing a *burqa* (see Figure 7)? Does it make a difference if the ban attaches not to clothing but to alcohol, or to illegal narcotics, or to the possession of components of nuclear or biological weapons?

International law has traditionally given the primacy to the right of a State to regulate conduct within its own territory. This is, of course, a solution driven largely by common sense and expediency. The practicalities are obvious. The person concerned, the people most directly affected by the person's conduct, the evidence of any crime, and the physical presence of the police and other authorities will all be in the territorial location of the conduct. Because law enforcement is necessarily local, it is impractical not to allow the law of the place where the conduct occurs to have immediate priority. But it is also a matter of principle: to let the national law of the individual govern the matter within the State where the conduct occurs would contradict the principle of the

7. **When municipal laws collide.**

sovereign equality of States, upon which the international order is built. Subject to limitations imposed by human rights law, each State has the right to choose to prohibit certain kinds of conduct, no matter what other States may think. Of course, the question whether it is wise or even justifiable to do so is an entirely different matter. International law sets the limits to a State's jurisdiction, but it does not stipulate how the State must exercise that jurisdiction.

When an individual returns, his national State may take steps to prosecute in respect of conduct in which he engaged abroad, even if that conduct was lawful where it occurred. Treason and similar offences are becoming topical examples again: persons who have participated in terrorist activities or training abroad may be prosecuted on their return.

There are conflicts of policy that can cause difficulty to individuals caught between conflicting legal demands, or even caught in situations where one law forbids them to do something that they have a legal right or a freedom to do under another law which is applicable to them. The US antitrust laws and other trade laws that conflict with the legal regime in other parts of the world have already been mentioned as examples. When such situations arise the tendency is to deal with them initially on a pragmatic basis, by consultation between the authorities in the States concerned. Prosecutions and the imposition of regulatory controls are discretionary steps, and if State A can give a good reason for asking State B to refrain from penalizing conduct—for example, that most of the evidence relating to the offence is in State A and that State A intends to prosecute the suspected offenders—the authorities in State B will often decide not to exercise their jurisdiction, unless there is some particular reason for insisting that State B will pursue the matter. Such steps may not resolve the issue of principle, but they may at least limit the enforcement of contradictory laws to cases where the States concerned consider that it is imperative that they act.

In a growing range of areas, however, there is sufficient commonality of interest for States to agree upon principles allocating jurisdiction. No State is likely to declare publicly that it wishes to protect the interests of narcotic traders or terrorists, for instance: all will say that they wish those activities to be controlled. Thus, there are treaties concerning certain types of terrorist activity, such as hijacking of ships and aircraft, hostage-taking, indiscriminate attacks, and the financing of terrorist operations, which require that the States Parties establish their jurisdiction over specified offences and take steps to enforce their laws in defined circumstances. Many such treaties utilize the *aut dedere, aut judicare* principle. Similarly, there is a slow move towards agreement upon basic policies and principles in areas such as environmental law and economic law. Where all States (or all States Parties to the treaties in question) apply essentially the same rules, it matters much less which of them actually applies its laws in any given case.

Beyond, but not above, the law

Bookstores in Washington DC used to sell a Diplomatic Licence Plate Decoder, which enabled concerned residents, enraged at illegally parked diplomatic cars, to direct their anger in an appropriate direction. Most capital cities have residents suffering similar frustrations. The immunity enjoyed by foreign diplomats, and the more restricted immunities enjoyed by their staff and families, are designed to ensure that diplomats are not harassed by local authorities and to facilitate the discharge of their official functions; but that does not extinguish a widespread belief that diplomats are effectively above the law. That belief is compounded by the fact that local police have no right to enter or enforce the law within the embassies of foreign States. Thus it is that London police were stationed for years outside the Embassy of Ecuador, where WikiLeaks founder Julian Assange took refuge in June 2012. Mr Assange, who is not a diplomat, faced immediate arrest and extradition to Sweden if he stepped outside the inviolable premises of the Embassy.

Foreign diplomats and consuls are not above the law; but they are beyond the reach of the police. Under the Vienna Convention on Diplomatic Relations they enjoy specific exemptions from taxation and municipal dues—and the dispute over whether the London Congestion Charge is, as some foreign embassies maintain, a tax or, as Transport for London maintains, a permissible charge for services rendered, led to £82 million in unpaid fines on diplomatic cars during the first decade of the daily charge. But apart from such specific exemptions they are subject to the law and obliged to obey it like all others. What they are not subject to is the enforcement of the law. Diplomats may not be arrested or detained; diplomatic premises may not be entered; and diplomatic property may not be seized. If a diplomat is accused of committing a crime, the solution is to expel him or her, by declaring them *persona non grata*. In practice, miscreants are often sent home by their own authorities in order to avoid embarrassment.

A similar immunity from the enforcement of the law is enjoyed by States. States cannot be compelled to appear in national courts; their property cannot be seized, in the way that the property of private individuals can be seized to satisfy debts; and States cannot be fined or subjected to court injunctions. At a time when governments confined themselves to politics and government, and were essentially the instruments of the power of the sovereign, notions of the equality of sovereigns (and later, the sovereign equality of States) provided a reason for not forcing any State to comply with the laws of another.

State immunity used to be absolute, so that a State could not be sued for anything; but over the past century States have increasingly engaged in what is in fact plainly commercial activity. If a company supplies cement for the building of houses or factories, it seems unfair that they should be able to sue on their unpaid invoices if the supplies were bought by a private contractor but not if the concrete was purchased for the same project by the government. If a shipping line or airline damages goods that it has contracted to transport, why should it be immune from being sued if it is State-owned but not if it is privately owned? This question became more significant with the rise of the centrally planned economies in States such as the USSR and China, many of whose industries competed in world markets. Western States began to adopt legislation withdrawing immunity in cases arising from commercial transactions, preserving it only for the 'public', governmental acts of the State. Though difficult questions remain, such as the classification of transactions that have a commercial character but a 'public' purpose (the buying of boots for the army is commonly given as an example), the international consensus now supports this notion of 'restrictive immunity'. It has become the general rule of customary international law, reflected in a Convention on the Jurisdictional Immunities of States adopted by the UN in 2004.

Jurisdiction: a major tool of international law

Jurisdiction is the conceptual framework within which States get things done. It marks out the limits of each government's authority and legal power to regulate behaviour and to rule; and it enables governments to construct arrangements by which they can cooperate in achieving common goals. It secures their right to independence, and is the vehicle of their interdependence. It divides all, and unites all.

Chapters 6 and 7 address the question of the limitations on what States can achieve by using this framework. Just because a particular goal is good, it does not follow that it is useful to try to enforce that goal by making a law obliging people to pursue it; and just because there is a law, it does not means that it is useful to try to enforce it on every possible occasion. Law does some things well and some things badly, and the lawyer, like other craftsmen, is wise to work with the grain.

Chapter 6
What international law does well

Law works best where it expresses aims and values that are already firmly and generally held throughout society—where its role is to formalize and order people's behaviour, rather than to change it. The point is obvious, and no reason for disappointment. Little of the pain and misery in the world is the intended result of deliberate policies. Most results from lack of will, resources, or foresight.

There is an ambivalence in most reflection upon the state of international relations. On the one hand, there is the tendency to suppose that, as the Liberation theologians said, we must each drink from our own wells. People must fight for their own freedom and their own future, because outside intervention usually fails, and if it succeeds it generally leads to some new form of colonialism. What point is there in providing foreign aid, or in toppling a regime, if the country is so riddled with corruption and nepotism that the only result is to entrench another ghastly kleptocracy? What good is done by fighting to protect people from a government or insurgent regime if the protectors subsequently leave the country and it reverts to its previous condition? Why not let people get on quietly with their own lives? Why can we not cut the ties that bind us to foreign interests?

On the other hand, there is a more communitarian view. How can we leave terrorists to do their work in the Middle East, or disease to ravage African countries, when the dangers will soon arrive on our doorstep if they are not stopped? Would there be so much of a problem with people-trafficking and illegal migration if poverty and discrimination in the countries of origin were addressed? Cannot the burdens of addressing the problem of global warming be spread fairly between States?

International life is carried on between the extremes of isolationism and internationalism. We try to help our fellow human beings in some ways, at some times, and in some places; but we do not actually take overall responsibility for their welfare. Governments do help each other, but because they choose to and not because they feel obliged to do so: the first loyalty of a government is always to the people who could remove it or cut off its supply of money; and it is probably fair to say that if a foreign problem can be ignored, most governments will be inclined to ignore it. There is, nonetheless, a degree of international cooperation that may be surprising, and that raises the questions of the circumstances in which States choose to cooperate and the ways in which they do so.

The broad point is clear: States cooperate in making and applying international law in circumstances where they are agreed upon the goals to be pursued, so that the law is employed to express a willing cooperation between them rather than to force rules upon them. Indeed, perhaps the only rules of international law that can really be said to be imposed upon States against their will are peace treaties imposed by the victors (which have tended to give way in modern practice to more cooperative transitional arrangements between the entities concerned) and, at least arguably, the terms on which international bail-outs are made available to States staring into the abyss of bankruptcy. In other areas States agree, even if grudgingly in the face of domestic or international pressure, to enter into cooperative arrangements.

Why and how States cooperate

The mechanisms of agreement can take different forms. There are some matters on which all, or practically all, States genuinely take the same position. The idea that torture is unacceptable is an example. There may be differences as to what actually amounts to torture: the debates over water-boarding were the product of such differences. There may even be a mental reservation that would reluctantly regard torture as permissible as a last resort in an extreme situation such as the 'ticking bomb' scenario; and the list of States Parties to the UN Convention Against Torture certainly includes a number which are reputed to resort to torture. But no State will actually speak out in favour of maintaining a legal right for States routinely to engage in torture.

Then there are matters on which States do not particularly care what rule is adopted as long as there is a rule, in the way that within a State it is necessary to reach a decision, however arbitrary, on whether to drive on the right or the left of the road. There are many international agreements on technical standards, from the precise definition of a metre and a kilogram, and navigation rules and signalling codes for ships and aircraft, to labelling specifications for food and drugs, which illustrate this phenomenon.

There are also matters on which States do have firm views on what rule should be adopted, but nonetheless consider that it is better to have a compromise agreement on one rule rather than a free-for-all or a muddle of conflicting rules. Agreements between interested States to limit fish net sizes for conservation reasons, or to set design specifications for ships and aircraft that will be accepted as 'safe' by ports and airports worldwide, or to fix purity standards for food and drugs, are examples.

So, too, are the many conventions that harmonize national laws on various legal questions, such as the rules on the validity of wills and testamentary dispositions and on the validity of contracts: the acceptance of common rules makes it easier to give effect to legal transactions of individuals that have some international aspect. A familiar example is the Warsaw Convention for the Unification of Certain Rules Relating to International Carriage by Air, which sets out agreed rules on matters such as the extent of the liability of airlines for lost or damaged luggage: the Warsaw Convention is commonly referred to on air tickets. This is the domain of private international law (or 'the conflict of laws', as it is often known). Private international law is the body of rules within each national legal system that determines which State's civil laws apply to relations between private parties that have a 'foreign' element—for example, whether a marriage celebrated in Italy by a Scots man and an English woman is governed by Italian, Scots, or English law; or whether a contract between a US company and an Indian company to deliver goods and services to a project in Egypt is governed by the law of a US state, or of India, or of Egypt. Private international law focuses on the rights, duties, and powers of individuals under civil law, and is made up of rules within each system of national law. Public international law, in contrast, focuses on the rights, duties, and powers of States, and on the reach of their public power expressed in, for instance, their criminal and tax laws; and it is made up of rules of international law such as treaties and customary international law. Thus, each national legal system—English law, French law, etc.—has its own rules of private international law, but harmonizing treaties developed by organizations such as the UN Commission on International Trade Law ('UNCITRAL') and the Hague Conference on Private International Law are doing much to alleviate the practical problems that arise from differences between national laws which might lead to inconsistent answers to legal problems depending upon whose courts hear the dispute.

These examples indicate something of the considerations that tend to produce more international agreements in some fields than in others. Of course, there are intermediate cases, and other reasons for States to be keen to reach agreements; but the making of most international agreements reflects one or other of the circumstances described above.

Equally, the shared interests naturally tend to draw States into compliance with many of these agreements once made. Why, for instance, would a State wish to mislabel exported foodstuffs, knowing that routine checks would discover the fact and probably lead to the withdrawal of the goods from sale and to the refusal of the buyer to pay for them?

There are, however, circumstances where it may pay one State to break the agreed rules while others observe them. Limits on fish catches are an example. If everyone else observes the rules while State A does not, there is likely to be an increasingly healthy fish stock which benefits State A while it makes no contribution to the task of conservation and fishery management. This is the 'free rider' problem. State A takes the benefit: everyone else pays the price. The free rider problem is one reason why international standards have an inherent tendency to be rather lax. If standards are too strict, some States may not sign up to them at all. It is better to have standards that are loose enough for all the important participants in the activity to accept, so that all of the key States are at least bound by some standards, than to have stricter standards and find that some States refuse to accept them.

A final point on the reasons why States agree. Though it is sometimes thought that law should prohibit everything that is bad, most people realize that law is an exercise in the art of the possible. It is pointless laying down rules that cannot be complied with relatively easily. Environmental law offers a clear illustration. Universal agreement on a ban on the use of CFCs in aerosols was achieved in the 1987 Montreal Protocol on Substances that Deplete the Ozone Layer; but agreement on significant action to prevent climate change is elusive and still seems far off. Why? The answer is that the ban on CFCs was adopted only when commercially attractive alternative propellants were available to buyers, and manufacturers could switch to other products. While not wholly painless, the implementation of the ban was clearly both practicable and efficacious in serving the intended objectives of the ban. In the case of climate change, the costs of action are very high and would be unevenly distributed between States, and there is still doubt as to the efficacy of any particular measures. Finding a compromise is proving correspondingly difficult: it is easier to agree that something must be done than to agree precisely what it is, and when it shall be done, and by whom, and who will pick up the bill. Moreover, the action that would be necessary to implement any agreement would spread across the whole of social life—transport, energy, taxation, trade, urban planning, and so on—and is not within the remit of any single government department, so that it is correspondingly difficult for States to define their negotiating positions and to send negotiators with the authority to agree even to tentative compromises. As the UN Special Envoy for Climate Change put it after the 2014 Lima round of negotiations, there is enough progress 'to keep the multilateral process alive, but not enough progress to give confidence that the world is ready to adopt an equitable and ambitious legally-binding climate agreement'.

Facilitating cooperation

The examples mentioned so far all envisage prescriptive agreements: that is, agreements to adopt rules or standards requiring people to do or not do certain things, to which the States Parties are bound to conform, whether it be the proper labelling of jam jars or the prohibition of torture or slavery. These are, however, not the only kinds of international cooperation. Some arrangements are facultative, and designed to facilitate transactions rather than to prescribe rules or standards.

Cooperation between legal systems is one example. There are treaties on the reciprocal recognition and enforcement of judgments, for instance, which ensure that a judgment given by a court in one State Party will be given effect by the courts of another as if it were one of their own judgments, and with a minimum of formalities required. Other conventions provide for the service of legal documents abroad, and for mutual assistance between States in the gathering of evidence for the pursuit of criminal matters and tax investigations, and for access to social security and medical assistance. The Council of Europe is particularly active in this field. Apart from the European Convention on Human Rights it has produced around 200 other treaties, all designed to facilitate 'common action in economic, social, cultural, scientific, legal and administrative matters'. Specialized international bodies, such as the World Intellectual Property Organization and the World Health Organization, adopt treaties and other instruments within their own fields of action.

There are also arrangements that are focused on the provision of a forum for discussion, rather than on the laying down of the terms of a particular mechanism to address a problem of common concern. Thus, treaties establishing international organizations must be counted among the instances of international cooperation secured by international law.

The most obvious example is the United Nations. Its main function is simply to be there, rather than to do anything. It is the place where diplomats from around the world gather and can discuss anything that they choose. It is the site at which countless international understandings are arrived at and agreements and decisions on courses of action are made. The proportion of these that are ever recorded as resolutions, let alone as binding treaties, must be tiny: but the understandings and agreements are immensely important. No treaty is necessary to underpin coordinated military interventions such as the 'coalitions of the willing' that have been such a striking feature of the post-Cold War era, for instance.

The range of international organizations is enormous: the Brussels-based Union of International Associations ('UIA') lists over 66,000 of them, including dead and dormant bodies. Most (including the UIA itself) are non-governmental organizations, but there are upwards of 5,000 intergovernmental bodies. Many specialized international organizations admit States that are not (yet) Members of the UN itself. For instance, UNESCO—the UN Educational, Scientific and Cultural Organization—includes among its 195 Members Palestine and Niue, neither of which is yet a UN Member State. It is usual in international organizations for each State to have the same number of votes, regardless of its size or power—thus in UNESCO, Niue has the same number of votes as China, whose population is more than one million times the size of Niue's; but exceptionally some organizations have systems of weighted voting. The IMF and the World Bank and the EU are the most notable, where the relative sizes of States' votes reflect the economic power or importance of the States. In the IMF, for instance, the USA has 421,961 votes (16.75 per cent of the total), compared with China's 95.996, the UK's 108,122, and Tuvalu's 755.

These instances of international cooperation between States have in common that the benefits of cooperation outweigh the costs. Cooperation is, generally, not an exercise in altruism, but an exercise in enlightened self-interest; and some areas of international activity are more susceptible to this than others.

What States agree upon

Even a skim through some of the 2,600 volumes of the *United Nations Treaty Series*, available online, will reveal the immense variety of the treaties—bilateral and multilateral; local, regional, and global—that States have concluded since the middle of the last century. Other series, such as the *League of Nations Treaty Series* and the various national collections of treaties, contain many more from earlier years, some of which remain in force.

Any attempt to summarize this body of practice is bound to be somewhat arbitrary and distorted, but some focuses of international attention stand out.

Trade and economy

Arguably the most significant area of international cooperation is the international economy. The 160-Member World Trade Organization ('WTO'), which succeeded the General Agreement on Tariffs and Trade ('GATT') under the 1994 Marrakech Agreement, is the institution at the heart of a network of more specific agreements that define the principles upon which around 95 per cent of world trade is conducted. States were able to balance concessions in one area against gains in another so as to produce an overall package acceptable to the WTO members, governing not only tariffs and import restrictions but also matters such as subsidies, technical barriers to trade, rules of origin, sanitary and phytosanitary measures, and (more controversially) trade-related aspects of intellectual property rights. The WTO also administers the much-used Dispute Settlement Understanding, which provides for adjudications by dispute settlement panels upon allegations of violations of trading rules, including high-profile disputes over matters such as the EU ban on the marketing and importation of meat products treated with hormones.

Agreement on these matters has been hard won, and the WTO practice of adopting measures by consensus rather than by majority vote has often threatened its ability to play as active a role in the development of international trade policy as many would wish. Nonetheless, the framework that it has already installed is a considerable achievement.

The trade framework is complemented by the international monetary system, where the IMF oversees currency exchange regulations and the World Bank Group provides support for major projects in developing and transitional countries. The practice of attaching conditions to World Bank loans has provided an

113

important mechanism for reinforcing international rules: for example, support for major dam projects has been made conditional upon compliance with international environmental standards. IMF conditionality has been more controversial, with accusations that the IMF has been used as a vehicle for the promotion of western economic policies of questionable utility to developing economies. Nonetheless, these bodies, and associated institutions such as the various regional development banks, and the so-called Paris Club and London Club which provide forums for the renegotiation of international debt, have done much to facilitate international trade and promote economic interdependence.

There are other treaties, too. Bilateral treaties for the promotion and protection of investments, measures to ease the integration of intellectual property rights into the trade framework, and harmonization measures have already been mentioned; conventions on international transportation, and on the movement of workers across frontiers can be added to the list. International law works well in this context because, while many of the obstacles to international trade flows may be the results of protectionist policies, the obstacles tend to take legal forms—either direct regulations on matters such as exchange controls, or obstacles that are the indirect results of divergences between national legal regimes. Both lend themselves to legal solutions in situations where goals, such as the relaxation of restraints on trade, are clearly defined and generally accepted. International organizations such as the International Labour Organization, the International Civil Aviation Organization, the International Maritime Organization, and the many bodies concerned with the infrastructure of transportation and telecommunications also perform a crucial role in oiling the wheels of international commerce.

Humanitarian law and human rights

A second area where international law has had considerable success is that of humanitarian law and human rights.

Humanitarian law is one of the oldest parts of international law, and the general desire of governments to avoid unnecessary suffering in warfare is a frail but vital thread running throughout its history. People like to think that they have right on their side when they use force against others, and that they can avoid senseless violence. The *jus in bello*, considered in Chapter 4, springs from that concern; and there is no doubt that by clarifying and reinforcing the demands of professional military discipline it has made a very important contribution to the mitigation of the suffering and waste caused by war.

The great global and regional human rights instruments of the United Nations era are also impressive achievements. Of course they are not always observed; of course they assert in stark terms very broad rights that probably could not ever be completely fulfilled. But the important thing is the articulation of internationally agreed standards against which the conduct of States can be measured. For the past seventy years no government could maintain that international law is irrelevant to the way that a State treats its own nationals, or that no State has the right to interest itself in such matters. The apparatus of regional human rights courts, international criminal courts, and supervisory committees to which States report (e.g. the UN Committees on aspects of human rights such as torture, the rights of the child, discrimination against women, the rights of migrant workers, and the rights of people with disabilities) keeps the subject in the thinking and policy-making of States.

Urban myths concerning human rights, of the 'man escapes deportation because he has a pet cat in the UK' variety, sometimes peddled by politicians who should know better, are misguided. Most of them are simply incorrect; but even if there is a grain of truth in some of them the solution must surely be for national authorities to apply international human rights standards more intelligently, and not to abandon the idea that there are some kinds of conduct that cannot be tolerated in any civilized society, even if some governments do try to engage in them behind drawn curtains.

Environmental protection

A growing body of evidence demonstrates the scale of the environmental and ecological threats that face humankind. Global warming, the destruction of natural habitats, and the alarming rate at which species are becoming extinct are problems that are now a routine part of primary school education around the world. It is an area where international law has chalked up some significant successes.

Pollution is no respecter of national borders; and any serious attempt to control anything more than local pollution within a State requires international cooperation. In order to bring about that cooperation, several factors need to be brought together: a common perception of the problem; a technologically sound and economically viable solution capable of making a significant contribution to the alleviation of the problem; and, in most cases, an understanding that the costs and benefits of action will be spread between States in a broadly equitable manner. Those factors have come together in several areas.

Marine pollution is one. Advances in ship design and equipment made possible a great reduction in pollution from both deliberate and accidental discharges of oil and other pollutants, and that potential benefit was realized by the adoption and implementation of a series of international agreements under the auspices of the International Maritime Organization. The agreements managed to phase in the new technology in an orderly and affordable manner, and to do so for the vast majority of world tonnage so that rogue shipowners would not be able to offer cheaper services and undercut the market by operating sub-standard ships. International law reinforced the agreements on design and operating standards through further agreements which coordinate the activity of port authorities around the world, ensuring that ships engaged in international trade are inspected frequently by one or other port along their voyages, and are effectively monitored for compliance with international standards.

There are comparable success stories in the field of ecology. Conventions that regulate fishing and hunting have preserved many species in the face of over-exploitation and the real danger of extinction. The adoption in national and commercial planning of concepts such as 'sustainable development', generated and refined by the UN World Commission on Environment and Development and similar initiatives, has given a readily understandable shape to environmental concerns and to the design of strategies to address environmental problems. Treaties such as CITES—the Convention on the International Trade in Endangered Species of Wild Fauna and Flora (see Figure 8)—and the Convention on Biological Diversity have had a great and beneficial influence upon the development of environmental controls. There can be few major civil engineering projects in the world now where the contractors or the funders or the host governments do not conduct environmental impact studies as a routine part of the project planning, for instance.

8. Repressing the illegal trade in ivory.

These examples illustrate a key point. The main value and practical impact of international law and international standards do not lie in decisions of international courts or tribunals or in resolutions of international organizations: they lie in the internalization of the rules and standards by governmental and private bureaucracies around the world, so that compliance becomes second nature. That is as true in the development of trade policy and humanitarian and human rights law as it is in environmental law. Indeed, it is true across practically the whole range of international activity.

Crime and punishment

A fourth focus of successful international cooperation is the repression of criminal activity. Crimes such as drug trafficking, money laundering, corruption, the counterfeiting of goods and medicines, cybercrime, and terrorism can only be dealt with by cooperation between national authorities; and international law is the natural vehicle for the protocols and understandings that secure such cooperation. INTERPOL, with 190 member countries, maintains a global network connecting national police forces, and facilitates cooperation between them on a day-to-day basis. The UN Office on Drugs and Crime is more concerned with the development of strategy and policy in relation to specific kinds of criminal activity of particular concern. And many of the treaties that have been drafted to overcome jurisdictional obstacles to the prosecution of international crimes also provide for cooperation between national authorities.

This is another area in which the law is well placed to facilitate international action because so many of the difficulties are themselves legal in nature. Piracy is a good example. Several European navies cooperate in policing waters in the Indian Ocean in order to deter or arrest pirates. Piracy has long been established as an 'international crime' which can be prosecuted by any State that arrests a pirate on the high seas; but it is simply impractical for, say, a British warship to sail back to the UK to hand over every pirate whom it might arrest for trial in the UK. It makes more sense to try the accused person in a nearby coastal State. But for that to happen the arrest must be carried out and the evidence collected in the manner required by the law of the State where the trial will take place. Furthermore, since the accused would be handed over by British authorities for trial, those authorities must be satisfied that the conditions of the trial and punishment are consistent with the UK's obligations under human rights treaties. International agreements settling appropriate procedures have made possible the trial of accused pirates by States such as Kenya, so as to enable international efforts to address the problem to proceed. The agreements are, of course, no panacea. The considerable cost to Kenya, and the social and economic conditions that foster piracy, are among the more obvious problems that also have to be addressed; but the alignment of the legal rules and procedures is a necessary step in clearing the way for practical cooperation.

The list of examples could go on and on; but there is little value in extending it. The point is that international law is best thought of as a way of doing things; and practically any kind of international arrangement that can be put into words can be made into law, and the arrangement fixed for future reference. There are, however, some things that international law does not do well, and it is to those that Chapter 7 turns.

Chapter 7
What international law does badly (or not at all)

International law is essentially a language (like a computer programming language) for recording agreements between States on principles and goals. Once the agreement is reached, writing it into law in the form of a treaty or inferring it from State practice as a rule of customary international law is not particularly difficult. And once the rule is articulated, the degree of compliance with it is usually broadly satisfactory. A skilled international lawyer can identify the critical areas of common ground, and lace them together with appropriate mechanisms for monitoring compliance and settling disputes so as to produce a robust legal regime to facilitate the implementation of the agreed principles and goals. But international law cannot manufacture agreement where none exists.

For this reason, international law is not well suited to the promotion of innovative solutions to international problems where the interests of States are radically divergent. That is the case in relation to climate change, and to the protection of commercial interests in proprietary drugs, for example. A developing State may take the view that its economy must be allowed a period of growth using old and relatively 'dirty' technologies, such as the developed world enjoyed through the two centuries following the Industrial Revolution; and it may consider that if there is an urgent human need for new drugs that it could manufacture and sell cheaply as generics, it should be permitted to do so. A developed State may take the view that the burden of averting an environmental disaster must be shared by all States, in a way that does not significantly upset the relative competitiveness of different economies; and it may consider that unless pharmaceutical companies can recover research and development costs by taking high profits from drugs during the limited life of their patent monopolies, research and development will dry up, to the detriment of the companies and of public health generally.

It is not the job of the lawyer to resolve debates such as these. Lawyers may be able to craft the terms of a legal obligation that provides for the phasing in of environmental controls on a timetable linked to the economic prosperity of the host State and the accounting write-down treatment of old plant and equipment, or devise a formula to define the circumstances under which a State may issue compulsory licences for the manufacture of patented drugs needed for use in an epidemic. But lawyers have no special ability or authority to decide whether any such solutions are or are not acceptable. That is a political choice. Most lawyers lack the expertise to say if such solutions would make economic or commercial sense—much less to give reliable predictions as to their effects upon employment or competitiveness.

Similarly, a lawyer can provide an answer to the question whether a particular military operation is or is not lawful as a matter of international law. But a lawyer has no special ability to say if there would be any moral justification for engaging in an operation that is lawful; much less can a lawyer say whether there would be sufficient military or political advantage in doing so. No matter how intense the debates over the legality of military action in Iraq or Libya or Afghanistan or anywhere else, that question should never be conclusive. Just because there is a right to do something, it does not mean that it is right to do it.

A related point is that international law cannot itself deliver international justice. Although its highest court is named the International Court of Justice, and the UN Charter insists on 'conformity with the principles of justice and international law' and the maintenance of 'international peace and security, and justice' as objectives, the currency of the international legal system is law, not justice. Thus, when deciding upon the boundaries between States at sea the International Court has made it clear that it considers that it cannot engage in corrective or redistributive justice. Poor States or States with short coastlines are not to be compensated by giving them a greater share of the seas adjacent to their coasts. Equally, ideas of unequal treaties or odious debts, according to which bargains accepted by States in the past can be overturned because their terms are regarded as so unfair as to be oppressive, have failed to take root in international law.

We transfer concepts such as justice, in any of its forms, from the national to the international stage at our peril. The difficulty of reconciling the duties of a democratically elected government towards its electorate and others who are within the State on the one hand, and towards citizens of other States and humankind in general on the other hand, is too great for it to be possible to make 'justice' a free-standing source of rights or duties in international law. International law may often be applied in circumstances where it appears that one State or another has to bear a burden not of its own choosing. A State unable to pay international debts because it has to deal with a famine at home, or where an ousted government has incurred massive debts through corruption or has embezzled State funds, may still be under a legal obligation to pay, no matter how great one's sympathy for the current government. The law can provide for the enforcement of legal rights and duties: the provision of aid and assistance to those who need it is a matter of policy. The law understands rights and duties; but it has difficulty with the concepts of compassion and forgiveness. While the law is an invaluable instrument for the implementation of policies that aim to make the world more just—the special preferential treatment given to developing States within the GATT and the WTO is a good example—it will not miraculously produce justice and fairness of its own force.

Nor can international law secure its own enforcement. If a State is set on ignoring its legal obligations, other States can impose sanctions upon it, and individuals may impose their own boycotts. But no law can itself compel a State to change its behaviour.

The law is an instrument; and lawyering is a craft. Neither can be pushed far beyond its natural limitations. This means that there are some areas in which, at least at present, international law is unlikely to be able to make much of a contribution to human welfare. International law will not reduce poverty or disease; it will not equalize life expectancies or incomes across the world, or access to water or to education. It can be used to express and give effect to the agreement of States to work towards these ends; but it cannot do more. The law can never establish a system so perfect that people do not need to be good.

Further reading

More detailed introductions to international law for non-specialists include *Brierly's Law of Nations* (7th edn, 2012, by Andrew Clapham) and my own *International Law* (2007). The collection of papers edited by Malcolm Evans, *International Law* (4th edn, 2014), is a thorough and advanced introduction to the subject that is particularly suitable for non-lawyers. The articles collected in the *Max Planck Encyclopedia of Public International Law* (published, and regularly supplemented and revised, online, and also available in hard copy) provide up-to-date and easily digestible accounts of a large number of key concepts. The *Introduction to Legal Research in Public International Law*, published online by the Institute of Advanced Legal Studies, and the Oxford Bibliographies *International Law* published online by OUP, are good starting points for further research.

Many books discuss international law from the perspective of international relations, though often more in the light of theory than of experience. Louis Henkin's *How Nations Behave* (2nd edn, 1979) is a classic text, still worth reading. Jack Goldsmith and Eric Posner's *The Limits of International Law* (2005) is an antidote to idealism, and perhaps to optimism. Philip Allot's extraordinary tract *Eunomia: New Order for a New World* (2001) offers a radically different and more hopeful view of international law and of its potential for making the world a better place.

Among the websites of particular interest to international lawyers are the network maintained by the United Nations <http://www.un.org/en/>, which has a specific section on the UN's work involving international law <http://www.un.org/en/law/>. Most other international organizations, such as the WTO <http://www.wto.org/> and the Council of Europe <http://hub.coe.int/> have their own websites. So, too, do the major international courts and tribunals, such as the ICJ <http://www.icj-cij.org/>, the tribunals organized under the auspices of the PCA <http://www.pca-cpa.org/>, the European Court of Human Rights <http://www.echr.coe.int/>, and the tribunals organized by the World Bank to hear investment disputes <https://icsid.worldbank.org/ICSID/>. Specific topics such as environmental law <http://www.unep.org/delc/EnvironmentalLaw/>, the law of the sea <http://www.un.org/depts/los/> and the law of armed conflict <https://www.icrc.org/en> have websites maintained by governmental or non-governmental organizations. In addition, general international law sites are maintained by many universities and associations. The sites of the American Society of International Law <http://asil.org> and the European Society of International Law <http://esil-sedi.eu> are particularly helpful, but by no means the only valuable sites.

Index

International Law

Index